NOTES ON THE ANICONIC

NOTES ON THE ANICONIC

The Foundations of Psychology in Ontology

Eric Rhode

Foreword by
James Grotstein

APEX ONE

First published in 2003 by Apex One
7 Hillsleigh Road
London W8 7LB

British Library Cataloguing in Publication Data

A C.I.P. for this book is available from the British Library

 ISBN: 0-9543231-1-4

10 9 8 7 6 5 4 3 2 1

Edited, designed, and produced by Communication Crafts

Printed in Great Britain by Biddles Ltd, *www.biddles.co.uk*

Contents

Foreword

James Grotstein

This is an utterly profound work. Eric Rhode seeks to explore a domain that has long been missing in psychoanalytic psychology: the ineffable domain of ontology or existence. He describes a multi-layered, numinous domain that engulfs the most ordinary reaches of our lives but has remained barely known to us.

His ideas are fascinating. His writings about transference and about the contact barrier make sense. He gets to the heart of the matter by counterpointing, as the mainstay to existence, the represented object with the unrepresentable "O". I appreciate the ways in which he thinks. In my understanding, the term "aniconic" literally means "without icons" and implies "beyond" as well as "before icons". The wisdom of the aniconic lies buried in myth and folktale and entails the most inchoate readings of "O". The content of these myths runs from fairy tale to sacred geometry. I was fascinated by the notion of the "axis", as in "axis

James Grotstein is Clinical Professor of Psychiatry at UCLA School of Medicine and Training and Supervising Analyst at the Los Angeles Psychoanalytic Institute/Society and Psychoanalytic Center of California.

mundi" ("axis of the world"), which suggests to me a whole new reading of the contact barrier in general and of the repressive barrier in particular. The function of the axis is to define the stabilising centre, so as to enable the experience of balance. "Being" and "Becoming" are the axials to metamorphosis and transformation.

One must read this work in the way in which Bion exhorted analysts to listen to analysands: "Do not listen to the analysand. Listen to yourself listening to the analysand." One must allow the "sense organ that is responsive to internal conditions" to be the reader.

Los Angeles

NOTES ON THE ANICONIC

A young goats-herd guarding his herd one day heard
unusual sounds. He did not know how they were caused.
Returning home to his father, he said, "I heard noises,
and I don't know how they were made." "Take some
pebbles," said his father, "and throw them in the
direction of the noise." The boy did this; *and whatever he
hit became visible.* [If a stone, when thrown, touches a
spirit from another world, it renders them impure and so
visible.] Several blacksmiths from the world of the
Yeban, who were using a sledge-hammer by a fire,
became visible. They brought their implements and fire
into the community.

Griaule, 1938: 49

1

Contact barrier & transference

> Spinoza once remarked (as Leibniz's friend Tschirnhaus
> told him) that the *vulgus* (the "common run": here, the
> Scholastics) took created things as their philosophical
> starting point; Descartes began with the mind; he,
> however, began with God (Leibniz, "Notes on a
> Conversation with Tschirnhaus", 1675, 385).
>
> Parkinson, 1989: 235 *n*69

Two presences are unavoidable in transference situations.
They are not limited to transference situations; and they
occur in situations that are not overtly transferential.
But it requires the intensity possible in the transference to
disclose their inseparability. They are like shadow and light.

One of them is an object of possible cognition—an "other"
that the self hopes to know and to engage with. Freud thought
that this object was realisable through the enactment of what
he called secondary process. His "Formulations on the Two
Principles of Mental Functioning" (1911b) describes how secondary process can transform the ego. The ego's capacity to test
the "reality" of the object of possible cognition increases its

1

ability to *think* and curbs its tendency for impulsive behaviour. By being able to *attend*, it is able to link up consciousness and sense information and to direct the sensory organs towards the external world. In secondary process, the ability to judge and assess somehow replaces the impulse to repress. The ego is able to deploy notation as a function of memory.

The existence of the object of possible cognition depends on its being an object that can be represented *and notated*. Its nature is such that it draws attention to memory as being of unusual importance, and to beliefs in a temporal repository for "that which has been".[1] It disavows the possibility that "the past" might be a concept of the imagination, a refraction into time of some unknowable and atemporal existence. It attempts to give to "the past" the appearance of a scientific fact.

The other presence in the transference is a type of transformation that Bion (1970) has described as "O", and which is definable (insofar as it is definable) as a verb-noun, rather than as a noun. "O" manifests itself as a *becoming*; and *becoming* is thought to derive from *being*; it is an ontological presence. The empiricist cannot investigate "O", although "O" may be the metaphysical base for empiricism. It is an existent without direct representation, manifesting itself through intuition and possibly anxiety, but "how" it manifests itself is open to conjecture. It is possible that it does not respond to "how" questions.

The history of transference could be written firstly in terms of an evolution towards the discovery of the object of cognition and secondly in terms of an evolution towards the discovery of the disjunctive transformations that typify "O" and that Bion describes as forms of catastrophic change.

The theory of secondary process postulates, without examination, that "that which is" is "that which can be represented". It does not bring into its orbit types of existence whose nature is such that they are without representation. It does not account for the fact that intuitions concerning transformations of the "O" type disable such secondary-process functions as notation, attention, and the making of judgements.

Freud's assumption that the mind in sanity will investigate the object of cognition does not address the question as to why any mind should open itself to the existence unconstrained by duration that Spinoza called *existence itself*: an existence that, since it has no need for the schemas of duration, has no means by which it can be represented and possibly has no need to be represented. The same question might be posed of those who seek to give a religious depth that cannot be directly represented to form in art.

A poetic symbol may articulate itself through the instrumentality of sequence, whether in space or time, but it need not operate in this way. For instance, the Hindu *yantra* is an inscape, a wrought object intended to focus spiritual insight, which by its power to concentrate thought anticipates the later discovery of optic magnification, whether by microscope or telescope. The *yantra* operates means of instrumentality that are not sequential; and although it makes use of extension, it appears to depend on a concept of metaphysical space that is different from the space of sensory apprehension.

In my view, the history of the concept of contact barrier, which originated in psychoanalysis as a neurological concept, and which then evolved into being some kind of membrane between different mental functions, has further evolved into a means for violent and inconsequential transformation. (The *becoming of "O"* gives rise to the religious institutionalising of "catastrophic change" in the form of *limens* and altars.) By this means, contact barrier is able to articulate spiritual insight. Its functionality is meaningful only insofar as it is used in the service of articulating the presence of the poetic symbol—a "form of life", to use Wittgenstein's phrase, that emerges unaccountably out of "nowhere" and just "is".

In his *Ethics,* Spinoza describes eternity as "without duration".

> I understand ETERNITY (*aeternitus*) to be existence itself, in so far as it is conceived to follow necessarily from the mere definition of an eternal thing. Explanation.—For such existence is conceived of as an eternal truth, just as is the essence of a thing, and therefore cannot be explained by duration or time, even though the duration is conceived of as wanting beginning and end. [Parkinson, 1989: 4]

The postulate concerning "that which is" as having to be "that which can be represented" depends on an unexamined assumption concerning some inherent metaphysical "rightness" in the subject–verb–object structure—as though a sentence structure of this kind existed, as of right, in congruence to some order in the cosmos.[2] It is this assumed "rightness" of sentence structure that informs the principle that the sane mind (subject) investigates (verb) the object of potential cognition. It is an assumption on which Renaissance humanism depends.

In the becoming-of-"O" type of theory, the concepts of subject and object disappear; and in their place there is a floating gerund-like state of affairs, which may be evidence of some post-catastrophic fallout. The gerund "becoming" is an example of this: signs appear out of nowhere and without seeming intention. They have become. Because I do not know how they have become, I might be inclined to think of them as hallucinations. In which case, I will think all creationist theories to be species of hallucination; that is, if I wish to claim that forms of meaning can arise out of a condition that I cannot comprehend. But my proposal is that the iconic, whose ground is the aniconic, communicates meaning differently from the hallucination. It might be asked: in what way do these signs differ from hallucinations? One answer might be: in terms of conjectures concerning pre-birth phantasy. For instance, I might describe a foetal perception of the placenta as being like a gerund or verb-noun in which the constituents of subject and object float.

Among the Minyanka people of West Africa (Jespers, 1979), there are two types of ritual burial: one burial is bound to the altar and involves three sacks containing *yapere*, or altar-fetishes, the other burial is of a jar containing the placenta. "Among the Minyanka, the placenta is the alter ego of the newborn. It is the silent witness of the 'first words' uttered *in utero* by the individual and, by analogy, of the first words registered in the divine matrix. It contains the signs that constitute the first creation" (ibid.. 82). The sacks represent "the sacred placenta out of which the universe was created" (Jespers, 1976: 117). "Our informants told us that all signs are signs of the anvil. The blacksmith, as master of initiation, is master of the sign" (Dieterlen & Cissé, 1972: 13).

Contact barrier is a concept that recurs in Freud and Bion, although fleetingly. An idea escapes from repression, the vibrant relic of an important and ancient idea, the gap–link between sky and earth in traditional cosmology, the horizon as some emerging third element. An indefinite expansion in space marks a point of transformation between a transcendental Being and an immanent Becoming.

Freud first referred to the contact barrier in a neurological context; and some commentators have described Freud's understanding of the contact barrier as anticipating Sherrington's definition of the synapse. The contact barrier is a means of insulation, and it is a means of facilitating communication between two neurones that are similar and yet incompatible when brought together. This picture lends itself (provisionally) to being personified as an imaginary mother who creates a type of enabling space in which imaginary twins—such as Tweedledum and Tweedle-dee—exist on either side of her.[3]

The contact barrier might have been a residual from Freud's pre-scientific self.[4] Conceivably, Freud had intimations of a structuralist problem that Lévi-Strauss exercises much later in his paper, "Do Dual Organisations Exist?" (1956). A floating signifier, or zero factor, reveals a dyad to be in fact triadic, by transpiring through the dyad structure. Alternatively, and moving away from Lévi-Strauss's formulation, it is possible to think of the zero factor as being one that absorbs the structure of the dyad into itself (the religious apprehension of some Holy Spirit as three in one and one in three). This would be to give Bion's "O" theory an absolute nature, which Bion might not have wished, and in which "O", as the transference or floating signifier, envelops any evidence of subject and object.

At much the same time as he posited the contact barrier, Freud wrote to Fliess about a strange phenomenon, which he saw as psychopathological and therefore related to a Freudian conception of untruth. I suspect that this is the first appearance, all be it split-off from Freud's definition, of the contact barrier as the site of catastrophic change. Certain hysterical patients, observed Freud, were terrified by some intimation of a gap: and this idea seemed to conjoin with another idea that appeared to have some property of intensifying, or even magnifying, the idea of a boundary.[5] I conjecture that, as the years passed, the separate meanings of the gap and the boundary modulated in Freud's thought and came together as the poetic symbol of the primal scene, which is a means of concentrating the significance of the transference and of giving focus to an aesthetic or spiritual apprehension, not unlike the Hindu *yantra*. I take Meltzer's evolution of the primal scene concept into the concept of combined object to be a further definition of the spiritual optic glass or *image in form*—to use Adrian Stokes's striking phrase—whose disposition is such that it can intensify spiritual insight, so that one sees a "pattern" that has no direct relation to the continuities of space and time. The poetic symbol exists in opposition to symbols of functionality; it is not an object of use and it cannot be used; it has an unpredictable and even wilful relation to means of duration. It has the waywardness of the Holy Spirit. When it has been forgiven for its behaviour, it can be described as "inspired", but from the functional point of view *tout court*, it will appear to be a form of hallucination and the essence of craziness. The death–regeneration space of the holy sepulchre is, from one point of view, craziness in its ultimate form, but from another point of view this metaphysical conception of space is the essential definition of the ground for transformation out of which the poetic symbol takes on being.

The essential, almost theological mystery in aesthetics since the time of Cézanne has been the problem of the plane surface. Why should the plane surface be in itself of such great value in the creation of signs, and why should it acquire under certain circumstances a depth that is different from the fabricated impression of depth in perspectival figuration?

If the gap and the boundary, as elements in a two-dimensional conception, become three-dimensional, then they show themselves to be an enclosure, whose walls are the intensified boundary idea and whose unknowable interior is the gap. The interior is inaccessible. Minds that think to intrude into this secluded space will either perceive a blankness or be overwhelmed by stimuli. No one can know what the interior might contain: a terrifying gap? the annihilation that ensues from witnessing the act of one's own procreation? the sacred void of the Holy of Holies? This is to look into an optic glass of an inside-out kind that reverses the instrumentality of the *yantra* and negates spiritual insight.

In the writings of Freud and Bion, contact barrier is the boundary between conscious and unconscious. There is an unknown—and something emerges from it, if only, as in the case of the primal scene, as an intimation. I would propose, however, that all these definitions of the contact barrier are ways of describing the transference, not as a facsimile theory, but as a matrix of some kind, possibly a matrix of the void. Out of this matrix arises temporality in the form of many systems of time.

A transformation that is not directly represented. Sequence, or time as a necessary order in linearity, is a prerequisite for representation. In order for representation to occur, there has to be duration. But in Spinoza's view, there may be a conception of existence that is unconstrained by the exigencies of duration and unhindered by an absence of any means that might be essential to representation.

That which cannot be represented may manifest itself through intermediaries, or through negations of an unusual impress. In transference situations, the threshold may take the form of a contact barrier that is unpredictable in its effect and possibly imperceptible.

In one respect, the contact barrier is a negation, insofar it brings about a transformation by means of a gap–threshold traversal across the spaceless and the timeless. This is the contact barrier as disjunctive transformer.[6] Duration and enduring are the basis of continuity, of sequence, and of the linear conceptions that determine the possibilities of representation. But in relation to that which endures, some notion of discontinuity—that is, of absence and loss—is required. Duration is always bound to its antithesis, which is breakdown—except in regard to the infinite.

You have to posit past and future to define types of continuity that cease, or that exist only as a potential beginning—and the past and future that you posit has to be specific. However, the authenticity of symbolic being, however tenuously related to duration and representation, is more true of intuition than the reality of past and future, as other than provisionally useful hypotheses, that "contain", perhaps spuriously, loss and discovery.

Spinoza describes as modal the type of thinking that requires concepts of past and future. "It is to the existence of modes alone that we can apply the term duration" (Letter to Meyer, in Shirley, 1995: 102). Modes are declensions from some fundamental (divine) substance. They are real, but they are not the real thing. They are not even attributes of the real thing.[7]

Notes

1. The trend by which notions of science and memory and history as "pictures which agree with actuality" came into existence is one that exists in opposition to Spinoza's conception of science as founded in the ontological.

2. Consider the relation between religious sentiment in ancient Egyptian thought and Jacob Polotsky's description of verb use in ancient Egyptian grammar, in which the "verb" appears to function quite differently from verbs in the Romance languages. Indeed, calling them "verbs" may be a misnomer.

3. In two-dimensional terms, the placenta in foetal phantasy is a maternal membrane that carries within it two constituents, father and son (sacrificer and the sacrificed), who are barely differentiated in enacting the roles of imaginary twins. They are essentially timeless.

4. I would suggest that it is the impact of the transference as a potent floating signifier that brings out the animistic implications of the contact barrier.

5. Freud describes the first stage of hysteria as "the *manifestation of fright* accompanied by a *gap* in the psyche". "Repression does not take place by the construction of an excessively antithetical idea but by the intensification of a boundary idea, which thereafter represents the repressed memory in the passage of thought" (1950 [1896]: 228). In this view, spatiality is intermittent and barely present. There is a *gap* accompanied by sensations of fright, the *intensification of a boundary* and a *primary idea* whose nature is *one of self-contradiction*.

In another, earlier letter, Freud refers to a "sexual scene" associated with early childhood (ibid.: 230). "The solution of hysteria lies in the discovery of a new source . . . phantasies" (ibid.: 244). "Everything goes back to the reproduction of scenes" (ibid.: 247). "The aim—in the *architecture of hysteria*—seems to be to arrive back at the primal scenes. In a few cases this is achieved directly, but in others only by a roundabout path, *via* phantasies. For phantasies are psychical façades constructed in order to bar the way to these memories. At the same time, the phantasies serve the trend towards refining the memories" (ibid.: 248).

6. *A condition of increasing unknowing:* this is the absolute negation of the divine king's alter ego, or the absolute negation of space within Christ's sepulchre prior to resurrection.

7. The aniconic radiates through attributes (thought and extension); it is present less directly in modes.

2

Icon

The theory of iconism is informative about the ways in which the contact barrier can be an agent for *existence itself*. Icon means "likeness" in ancient Greek, but the likeness is not a similitude; it is not a metaphor, which relates objects that are knowable. It relates an object that is incipiently knowable to an object that is not available for empirical enquiry; it relates the incipiently knowable to the unknowable. The key concept in this relation is duration, which must somehow emerge from the aniconic object without representation if it is to give form to the object that is incipiently knowable.[1]

In Genesis, man allegedly is made in the image of an unknowable God. In Plato's dialogue, the *Timaeus*, time allegedly is an image of an unknowable eternity. Image, in both these cases, is an icon. It places an emphasis on the image's relation to an unknowable source. It does not place an emphasis on the image's relation to a spectator; in this, it differs from an expectation, habitual in Western culture, concerning the object in representation as a function of the subject. The aniconic, which is the unknowable source, whether described as eternity

10

or as the sacred, can be presumed to generate the iconic; and it may operate by way of a demiurge, or agent, or contact barrier as an extension of the iconic process itself. In the syntax structure of subject–verb–object, verb and object may contract into each other if the subject should be unknowable. The object, as icon, is inseparable from the history of its making: it *is* its own making.

In the *Timaeus* a celestial demiurge is able to create the cosmos when the aniconic generates an ontological numerology, in the form of an iconic and sacred geometry. In traditional cosmology, the terrestrial creationism of the human artist can be concretely equated with the workings of the celestial artist.

The structural affinity of the Genesis and the *Timaeus* quotations is apparent if I personify them as pairs of imaginary twins. A human being and linear time find their reflection in an iconic human being and an iconic conception of time, whose source is inaccessible to cognition. Existing in sequence, the spectator looks into the icon as though to find an unexpected reflection and may become aware of forms in temporality that, in their emerging from the atemporal, are as diverse as the multiple forms of music.

Although the contact barrier is imperceptible, unpredictable, and largely without representation, it determines the representations available to thought. Before the discovery of the concept of zero, the ancient Greeks, in their concern with the ontology of numeracy, gave the status of zero to an object that they called "The One". Much in the same way as the idea of zero determines the fields of mathematics, so the contact barrier determines the fields of representation and influences the formation of three kinds of representation.

- *The thinker thinks his thoughts.* Subject–verb–object: the ego-thinks-the-object. Galileo's belief that the scientist reads nature like an encyclopaedia (in Koyré, 1957) characterises the first representation, although it does not do justice to the complexity of Galileo's own Platonist position concerning representation. The thinker is able to control his own thoughts and the object of his thoughts; indeed, he is able to create the object by thinking it. His thoughts either tally or they fail to tally with an actuality that is knowable. The thinker presumes that he himself is a knowability and belongs to this sphere of knowable thoughts; he believes that the nature of his thinking can be ascertained, and that the objects that he thinks about are unknowable.

- *Releasing the object into autonomy.* In the first representation, the thinker hopes to control the objects by a type of thinking that approximates to the uses of literacy. In order to release this object, the linguist Saussure (1916) had to separate the culture of speech from the culture of writing and to consider speech as one among other sign systems, and quite other than a text. Lévi-Strauss has applied Saussure's understanding of sign systems to the space of traditional cosmologies, and he has extended Saussure's understanding of zero function in sign systems to an understanding of zero functions in cosmic topographies. Language, like ritual, custom, and habit, are "forms of life", to use Wittgenstein's concept: they are to be investigated in themselves and for themselves. "Forms of life", as poetic symbols, arise seemingly out of "nowhere". In other words, they are icons that the aniconic generates. Within these circumstances, there is no place for the conception of mind as a means of mediation.

- *The fusion of the verb and object under the determination of an unknowable subject.* The unknowable, or ontological, thinks the thinker; the aniconic generates the iconic. Under the influence of the unknowable object, verb and object fuse and disclose themselves as iconic. In this type of cosmology, all beginnings are re-beginnings, and the Word as creation is always a resurrection. The act that creates the icon is the regenerative act of the sacrifice.

It is possible to respond to transference phenomena in much the same way as the African sculptor who thought of the forms of inspiration as revealed to him "like something coming to the surface of the water" (Himmelheber). The transference, as a

form of the contact barrier, is in origin aniconic. People catch on
to it like a net.

Notes

1. The views on iconism here elaborate on interpretations in Ladner
(1953) and Kitzinger (1954).

3

The invention of mind & body

Aspecific kind of anxiety derives from Descartes's arguments in his *Meditations* of 1641. Any attempt to correlate mind and body—if mind and body should be given definition as possible existents—appears to be equivocal; and any attempt to stabilise the correlation, say, by using the idea of God to underpin it, is liable to increase the tremor of impending catastrophe. Means of proof and the idea of God are incompatible, and attempts at proof, in failing to decrease the perturbation, increase the state of insecurity.

A contact barrier relates, and yet keeps separated, two possibly hypothetical entities—in this case, mind and body. *It is as though contact barrier as the correlation, which is the source of perturbation, had to invent mind and body, in order to realise itself.* In a similar way, it might be possible to say that "O" as a perturbing correlation had to bring into existence patient and therapist in order to realise itself. The strength of the belief that mind and body (or patient and therapist) give authority to the theory of identity by their qualities of particularity is an indicator of the intensity of the denial raised against realising the meaning of the correlation as a correlation.

In one interpretation, the contact barrier facilitates communication between the two entities by keeping them apart, as a
way of protecting them from each other. In another interpretation, it separates the two entities in order to insulate them from
itself. As gap as well as link, in this respect it is a prototype for
the idea of catastrophic change.

Mind and body have a way of taking over each other's pre-
rogatives. The "devouring" lies in part with them, and in part
with the nature of the correlation itself. Perturbation, and fears
of usurpation, derive less from the correlated mind and body
than from the nature of the correlation. Mind-ego and body-ego
as objects of identity are unable to restrain the perturbing
reality of that which correlates them.

It is the custom among the Kuna Indian women of Colombia
to stitch cloth panels, called *molas*, which they attach to the
backs and fronts of their blouses. An example of a *mola*, which
I have before me, shows two almost identical birds, who are
related to each other, and yet separated, by a patterning that is
evocative of a labyrinth. In terms of the contact barrier, the two
birds are Freud's neurones personified as imaginary twins,
while the labyrinth pattern, which relates and separates them,
is a representation of the vibrancy and incipient power of dis-
turbance, of a mother in her role as contact barrier between the
twins.

A mother of this mythic kind appears in scattered references
throughout Freud's writings, usually in relation to his writings
on literature. The mother's benign qualities of intercession
more or less "contain" her powers of annihilation (as in Freud's
understanding of King Lear's youngest daughter.) Comparable
to the enigmas of the sphinx, which is prominent in Bion's, if not
in Freud's, conception of Oedipus, she is related to rites of
passage, which enact the crossing of the gap of annihilation. In
the Punjab, at one time, midwives would show women in labour
a picture of a labyrinth, as a way of articulating the nature of
their journey through possible death into childbirth.

The structure *twin : mother : twin* contains within it the
counter-theme of *breast : gap (infant) : breast*. Donald Meltzer
has indicated that the neonate may discover a life-and-death
space as it travels from one feeding breast to another (personal

communication). The journey through the death that yields discovery by way of the valley between the breasts[1] may invoke the possibly depressive discovery of some, or possibly many, of the meanings of spatiality in dream—and it carries within it the potential for discovering imaginary siblings, who form out of this space concurrently with the formation of signs.[2]

Travelling from the first breast, the infant may discover in the space between the breasts the structures of traditional cosmology, as well as the multiple armatures on which any aesthetic encounter will depend. The forms of geometry and art manifest themselves out of the "nowhere" of the skin between the breasts. There is loss in leaving the first breast and a restoring sense of discovery in finding the second breast. It is as though the different breasts represented aspects of a mother's gaze.

> On tomb representations and on steles, the *shen* sign is commonly placed between the two *wadjet* eyes, corresponding to the midpoint of the cycle between the west (the right eye) and the east (the left eye). [Rambova, 1957: 36 *n*14]

The *shen*-circle is an emblem for the cosmos itself, as well as for the extensive powers of kingship. It indicates Re's encircling of the cosmos. An infant, travelling from one breast to another, may discover in the "blankness" between the breasts a similar example of sacred geometry as a *yantra* by which the imagination intuits the emergence of forms.

Certain rites in West Africa, concerning the entry of redemptive light into the earth (see *infra*), raise the possibility that the infant's capacity for insight concerning the nature of the space between the breasts derives from intuitions concerning the placenta as a plane surface. (This would be a way of formulating the genius of Cézanne.) The "twins" of the placental membrane, differing from natural twins, are like two spirits in one body, or two bodies inhabited by one spirit. They exist according to a logic that properly belongs to music. They are rudiments out of which emerges the structure of the sacrifice, in which one twin may appear as the father who devours the other twin as son, or in which the son (as the new year, marking the beginning of time), devours the ending of the year in the form of his father.

The devouring, which formerly had been an attribute of the mother as contact-barrier intercessor, moves into the relationship of the twins, making manifest a conception of time as devouring.

Descartes takes the relation *mind : perturbing correlation : body* and translates it into the relation *mind : God : body*. It is possible to translate the relation further by replacing the God concept with the concept of zero. The potency of zero transforms the grammar of the system by opposing any claims made for mind and body as systems embedded in duration as a universal. A tripartite system founded on zero is thus a system centring not on a father–son dualism but on a third element, which is grace or the Holy Spirit.

It is on this basis that I assume a common ground in the criticism by which Spinoza disowns Descartes's system and the criticism by which Bion disowns Freud's distinction between primary and secondary processes. Spinoza and Bion reject the claims to centrality of the ego-nucleus theory and they reject it by comparable means: in Spinoza's case, by his definition of existence itself, in Bion's case, by his evocation of the becoming of "O".

A poetic symbol, unlike body or mind, is a presence of otherness, or altereity, which eludes definition. It appears to arise from the often incoherent correlation between body and mind, or of self and the other: but it cannot be deduced or inferred from any attempted correlation. It exists as an alternative to the idea of a fact: it is a messenger of the imagination (or, in Coleridge's quasi-theological understanding, "the Imagination").

Spinoza mentions the concept of *existence itself* in passing and then lets it pass without further mention, while Bion refers to the becoming of "O", without explicating its meaning.[3] But there is enough to go on. In their separate ways, Spinoza and Bion call into doubt the notion of duration as a universal. The emphatic nature of bodily sensation endows the concept of event with authority; but this need not result in the body being an absolute yardstick for temporality.

Spinoza cuts through the otherwise unresolvable equivocations of Descartes's correlation of mind and body. In Spinoza's assertion, seventeenth-century presumptions about universality in physical law do not endorse any correlation of mind and body. Spinoza's assertion therefore undermines the system of psychological categorisation, based on seventeenth-century mechanics, which has sanity depend on the postulate of a universal notion of duration.

The ego nucleus creates a background against which it can envisage itself as being the foreground, by presuming that the idea of universal duration, which it discovers in itself, can be projected onto its environment. It exists against a backdrop that is identical to the conception that it has of its own internality. This is not the space of traditional cosmology, into which zero function is able to project many forms of space by way of many forms of temporality.

Notes

1. "The valley of the shadow of death" of Psalm 23.

2. I assume this space, with the mythic space in which signs form in the placenta, to be some of the forms of metaphysical space as defined by Plato.

3. Bion articulates the becoming-of-"O" theory in *Attention and Interpretation* (1970), but it is a theory the existence of which is implied throughout his later writings.

4

Beginnings

> They [possibly the Cartesians] have not observed the
> order of philosophical argument. For the divine nature,
> which they ought to have considered as prior in
> knowledge and nature, they have thought to be last in
> the order of knowledge. . . . Hence it has come about
> that, while they considered natural things, they paid no
> attention to the divine nature, and then, when later they
> directed their attention to the divine nature, they could
> think of nothing but their first fabrications on which
> they had founded their knowledge of natural things.
>
> Spinoza, *Ethics*, 2 *n*10

From the first page of his *Meditations*, Descartes is confronted by the hazards entailed in any enterprise that "begins with mind"—and he is inclined to think of himself as going insane. The problem lies initially in thinking in terms of a dualism (*mind : body*), then realising that the dualism conceals a further element, which is either an underpinning to the structure or the cause that will bring it tumbling down. In

19

other words, God performs the role of contact barrier in this argument, being an existent whose validation as an existent has to be "proved", so that it can endorse the truth of the *mind : body* distinction—in the form almost of an afterthought.

The tempestuous seas across which the Cartesian pilot attempts to sail his ego are those aspects of mind that are opposed to being controlled by the ego. Bion (1973: 16–17) describes the prospect of shipwreck in terms of Book Five of the *Aeneid*— Virgil's great study of rite of passage as death-into-life—in which the god Phorbas, disguised as Sleep, flings the steersman Palinurus headlong into the sea and then tears away the helm and part of the stern of the ship. The dead Palinurus is, unfairly, held responsible for this disaster. The incident outrages the natural order of things in a way that has to remain inexplicable—in the same way as any emanation of the poetic symbol cannot be explained. Any attempt to interpret the incident will diminish its communication of shock.

In Shakespeare's play *The Tempest*, which antedates Descartes's *Meditations* by about thirty years, Prospero just avoids drowning while escaping from the tyranny of his brother Antonio in a boat that leaks. Established on his isle, he himself cannot avoid tyrannical habits in thinking to use literacy magically as a way to exercise control over the inhabitants of the isle. By magic he brings Antonio, his bad brother, and Antonio's doublet, Alonso, King of Naples, to the isle, while failing to realise that magic will bring about his downfall, as well as the downfall of others. As a consequence of the shipwreck, Alonso's son Ferdinand arrives on the isle and meets with Prospero's daughter Miranda. The love that Ferdinand and Miranda feel for each other releases Miranda from her father's authority and modifies her father's desire to control everyone.

But, in addition to Prospero and Antonio–Alonso, there is a third brother, an imaginary twin, who brings into focus the play's depth in imagination. Alonso and the court were thought drowned in a ship that went down with all hands (which psychologically is an accurate way of describing the dilapidating worldliness of the court). In fact, Alonso has survived drowning and is as crooked and political as ever. But in the thoughts of his

son Ferdinand, who is aided by the spirit Ariel, the depths of the
sea have richly and strangely transformed Alonso's non-existent
and imaginary corpse. Ariel sings:

> Full fathom five thy father lies;
>   Of his bones are coral made;
> Those are pearls that were his eyes:
>   Nothing of him that doth fade
> But doth suffer a sea-change
> Into something rich and strange.

[Shakespeare, *The Tempest,* Act I, Scene 2, ll. 396–401]

The non-existing body of the king in transfiguration floats and
ramifies in a marine space, which engages with the non-existent
corpse of the king and transforms it, as a form of Freud's
"oceanic"—a concept that, perhaps inadvertently, had Freud
somewhat change his description of the unconscious. The space
in this mythic sea's depths is aniconic; in Plato's terms, it is
metaphysical. It has little or no relation to the kinds of space
that the senses or intuition register. Spinoza's unknowable *existence itself* provides a culture in which the poetic symbol can
come into being within imaginative spatiality, the space of
myth. If mind—and, possibly, body—are satellites of such a
kind of symbol, then they are ontological, rather than psychological, objects of enquiry.

Transference resembles a verb that does not require subject
and object; a floating signifier that literally floats; a gerund that
exists on the threshold of an existence without traces of duration
or of those types of existence that require spatio-temporal definitions. Presumably Freud apprehended metaphysical space, or
the oceanic as its derivative, before he defined the oceanic—for
metaphysical space and the oceanic are the essence of intuition
in the transference. Bion's re-founding of transference on "O"—
a foundation that is void rather than substructure—makes this
point plain.

The relation of transference to the dyad (*any* dyad) is fleeting. Within it, subject and object are like the transfiguring body
of a drowned yet non-existent king. Transference is like Robin
Goodfellow, who creeps into the darkened house where the

lovers sleep, in order to place his blessing on them. ". . . Not a mouse / Shall disturb this hallow'd house", he says in the concluding scene of *A Midsummer Night's Dream* (Act V, Scene 1, ll. 394–395).

Transference as poetic symbol presides over the place of consultation, whether or not anyone has ever entered the room.

5

The threshold between psychology & ontology

The contact barrier appears in Freud's writings in a disguised form, and possibly for the last time, in the notes dated June 1938, which were published posthumously (1941f [1938]: 299). Freud conjectures that apart from "Kant's *a priori* determinants of our psychical apparatus", the "psychical apparatus" may operate by other means. "Psyche is extended; knows nothing about it" (ibid.: 300).[1]

On the one side, as against awareness of the contact barrier, there are the *a priori* determinants—mind, or at least ego, containing its own powers of generation; reason as its own subject, bulwarked against the incomprehensible and confusing. On the other side, and in awareness of the contact barrier, there is a dissolution of the ego as a nucleus for thought, and an abandoning of a subject–verb–object type of sentence. The psyche in extension *floats*. The extension might be the source of the psyche, as well as the source of some meaningful *unknowing*; it is like light filtered through a stained-glass window. Silence and luminosity interfuse with the imperceptible iconic forms that define sonority and hue. When contact barrier reveals itself, the subject disappears—or, rather, it reveals its source to be aniconic and without any need for representation.

The nature of the non-existent king's body as a variable is similar to the indeterminate nature of its watery setting. It exists between the aniconic and the forming of the icon in a translucence that is suitable for a poetics of zero. Poetic symbols of this kind in painting can take the form of a luminosity that the art-work refracts, in music of a silence resonant within sonority. The painter and writer on the arts, Adrian Stokes, has written specifically about the blossoming of stone (beneath a carver's hand) and, generally, about the artist's need to elicit the *image in form*. Releasing the image in form is an act comparable to the release of luminosity on a painted canvas, or of music out of a silence conceived of as a matrix.

The composer and conductor Pierre Boulez has commented on the fact that among the many types of people who listen to music in an audience, there are likely to be those who are aware of the silence intrinsic to the forming of the musical notes. The quality of their attention contributes in an unusual way to the quality of the group reverie, through which members of the group listen to the music. The aniconic—in the form of luminosity, silence, or the oceanic—provides variables, which seem to make their entry into spatio-temporal systems almost discreetly.

Within this conception, music and painting are "forms of life"—which is a way of describing the inexplicable presence of the poetic symbol. Language is similar. As speech rather than as writing it just is there, shared, passed back and forth like an imperceptible ball in play. Its iconic quality draws attention to its source in the aniconic and to the need for some means of notation that can represent its substrate in the unknowable and the void. In the view of the linguist Saussure, who makes the point lightly, zero operates within sign systems as a means of reparation; it enables damaged or deteriorated systems to continue functioning. Saussure sees zero as a sign; he does not explore its potential as a symbol, which is usually disquieting. However, this larger view of zero as symbol is implicit in his awareness of the symphonic nature of speech systems. He conceived of "the whole Indo-European system . . . as a pure schema composed of elements which are defined entirely by internal reciprocal relations" (Hjelmslev, 1971: 84).

Zero as the means that enables deteriorating systems to continue working is contact barrier in its role as a facilitator of communication and a means of insulation between incompatible albeit similar elements. But zero can also represent contact barrier as the gap within the link, the element of catastrophic change that is disjunctive transformer. As a poetic symbol, zero can be an equivalent for an entire language. But it is also the site for sunk galleons, the void-foundation in the ocean's depths in which a symbol might originate.[2] If Freud's "oceanic" is an example of an unbounded saturate, then the poetic symbol is an example of such a saturate.

Aristotle's understanding of how a house is built (in Barnes, 1984: 333–334) is a model for a functionalist conception of mind (in which mind is assumed to have "*a priori* determinants"). It is a sensible form of building, which lays stress on the value of good foundations. It proposes an aetiology or theory of *how things come to be*, in which there is no place for such concepts as aniconic or iconic. Four or five "causes" account for the construction of a house. There is the *formal* cause (the architect's plans), the *material* cause (the material used in building the house), the *efficient* cause (the act of building), and the *teleological* cause (the end to which the house will be put). The causes or explanations for the house's existence are intrinsic to the house itself as forms of *causa sui*: a house is self-sufficient both as an explanation of itself and as a construction. There is no mystery about its building and no need to bind it into some imaginary cosmos of reciprocating acts of creation and sacrifice. If it should acquire the quality of a symbol, it does so by chance.

The notion of "psychical apparatus" as having "*a priori* determinants" establishes mind as a mental nucleus, whether in ego or primal scene, which asserts the primacy of itself as subject. Like the Aristotelian house, it consists of little other than its own history, which includes every form of nature and nurture (parents, genetic codes, experience, etc.). Etiological thinking of this kind considers links as tangible and metaphors as a means of anchorage. But mind as operating by extension, and as not knowing about its means of operation, no longer sees psychology as *causa sui*; it bases psychology in ontology; it realizes that all its imaginative structures must be founded in the void. Thus it engages with signs in some qualitatively different way from the way that mind does in its Aristotelian aspect. The assumption with which it receives signs is that they are continuously in transformation between the aniconic and the iconic, as agents for that which cannot be represented—which is also that which cannot be decoded or controlled.

The extension of the psyche has to be one that is bound up with a condition of unknowing. The blind man cannot see his hands as they stretch out in exploration; and indeed he may think of his hands as a negation of the intuition related to clouds of unknowing. The concept of mind as mirror image of itself disappears on any entry onto the threshold between psychology and ontology; and in its place appears cataclysm.

A composer might write a series of variations around a theme, which conceivably is hidden from him. The expectation of finding the theme might be the motive that activates the writing of such "enigmatic" variations. The contact barrier is a theme without representation, which generates many variations, even though the aspect of it that can be known is largely known as an indeterminate negation or unknowing, the act of sacrifice in the creationism of traditional cosmology. Mind, as subject, stretches out to actuality (its object); but if the verb (stretching out) should become the subject of the sentence, it will show itself to be an agent or contact barrier for an unknowable, an intercessor between sky (ontology) and earth (psychology). The contact barrier, as emblem of the sacrifice, as the means that releases the celestial into a terrestrial condition by way of multiple temporal schemas, communicates an impression of being like a meteor that, in being burnt up on entering the atmosphere, leaves only residuals of iron and stone on the desert floor. In mythic thought, the residuals are elements of an icon that could not tolerate conditions that were other than aniconic, as though it were a god who, in entering the terrestrial, could not survive in the atmosphere of the terrestrial. In ancient Egyptian ritual, sacred adzes, which broke open the mouth of the dead in ceremonies that were intended to enact rebirth, were forged from the metal of these residuals, as icons that restore the dead to the state of the aniconic.

Notes

1. *"August 22.*—Space may be the projection of the extension of the psychical apparatus. No other derivation is probable. Instead of Kant's *a priori* determinants of our psychical apparatus. Psyche is extended; knows nothing about it" (Freud, 1941f [1938]: 300).

2. In ontology the number one (hypostatised as the One) covertly assumes the grammar of zero in order that as sign/symbol it might generate numbers. But it originates nothing; as a sign, it can repair or destroy systems, or it can become a symbol for absolutely everything or absolutely nothing: but "nothing" (the pun is unavoidable) generates it; although it might appear to generate everything.

6

A calabash in fragments

While visiting the village of Yobri Sapiaga in Upper Volta, the anthropologist Michel Cartry observed broken bits of calabash gourd on the ground. On the concave side of the calabash bits were carved marks or signs (Cartry, 1963, 1976, 1978, 1981), which Cartry came to learn were the source for the signs that diviners drew on the ground in geomantic acts of divination.

The marks on the calabash bits differ from the marks that constitute writing. The fragmenting of the calabash indicates why. Writing depends for its significance on a continuous background; it requires a background of neutralised space, in order that it might occur; it requires controlled circumstances. The way in which its marks unfurl appears to endorse belief in there being only one state of affairs—a linear flowing forward in which duration is an exigency and reality sequential. Within this circumstance, temporality has to be a progression from past into future.

The assumptions on which writing depends observe the two Cartesian criteria for truth: being "distinct" (having a location) as well as "clear" (invoking sense impressions). But signs in general, and the sign thinking of West Africa in particular, have a different reality. Although "clear", they come into being by means of a setting that is indistinct: the interior surface of a calabash in bits communicates a problematic and dislocated idea of space.

Diviners who use divination in the practise of healing use the signs on the concave fragments to prescribe cures for sick people. The fragments represent illness concretely as a body in bits. The dislocation in space on which the signs depends is analogous to altars and temples as portals of death into regeneration. The body broken in sickness is evocative of the series *aniconic > act of sacrifice > iconic*.

Identifying with a broken object in order to understand its significance is similar to the Freudian need to blind oneself "artificially" in order to intuit an extension that psyche knows only as an "unknowing". It is to be in identification with a non-existent drowned body within the waters of the imagination and with the mysterious means by which the poetic symbol ramifies. Signs, and speech, are different from writing. Artificially blinding oneself to the uses of writing, so as to intuit the extension in unknowing or depth in spatiality on which sign systems depend, is to identify with a fragmenting in space that is indistinguishable from a fragmenting in body.

Cartry describes how the Gourmantché have two sacred circles: in one they practise the sacrifice, and in the other they practise the act of reading the signs of divination that appear on the ground. Conceivably, a passageway, passing through an indefinite space, links one circle to the other and points to their fundamental identity. It is by imperceptible means of this kind that the broken bits of body translate into the signs of divination, by which the future impresses itself on the present. In this version of contact-barrier theory, the contact barrier is like the indwelling spirit that separates one sacred circle into two circles, or one neurone into two neurones, much as the presence of Eve, as rib or *axis mundi*, separates the fused imaginary twins of father and son in the garden. The twin who undergoes dismemberment in the circle of the sacrifice and the twin who transmits the potency of the future into the present in the circle of divination are twins in name only. Between these two aspects of emerging individuality (which possibly are latent in every-one) is contact barrier as some iconic link between the one who conducts the sacrifice and the one who is the sacrificed. Geom-etry, as a form of the universal, arises in the imaginary space between the two circles. The void out of which these images in form arise is unknowable, because its potency is immeasurable, as well as being without representation.

The shallow ground on which writing depends maintains the grid of perspective. It locates the negation of the sacrifice at some "vanishing" point, behind the surface plane of the writing, whose distance behind the plane is commensurate with the distance of the spectator before the plane. But perception of signs, and their relation to the fragmented object, requires the psyche to arrive at a different conception of spatial depth, a form of extension that is related to states of "unknowing".

7

The indistinct

Descartes thought that a description had to be "distinct" as well as "clear", in order to be true. A phenomenon without a specific location had to be a delusional phenomenon. "I have heard that those who have had a leg or arm amputated sometimes seem to feel pain intermittently in the missing part of the body" (*Meditations*, in Cottingham, Stoothoff, & Murdoch, 1984, 2: 53). The acute pain in the patient's leg is indistinct, without sure location, because a surgeon amputated the leg yesterday. But the pain is "clear"—its effect cannot be denied. The patient locates the pain *nowhere*, in a phantom limb, thinking it *somewhere*. He requires someone with neurological information to explain to him why he has located pain in a phantom limb.[1]

The indistinct relates to not knowing the right location. In certain activities this is a disadvantage: the activities lose any meaning they may have had. But in activities related to the contact barrier, the indistinct can be an indicator about a truth concerning the nature of the spatial ground on which certain activities occur.

31

The paper that someone writes on has a different plane in psychic reality from the canvas on which someone paints. The writer can be confident that his marks will rest on the plane which he writes on; and in his confidence he can assume unselfconsciously that a plane exists which consists of invariable distances and out of which a map might be construed. The markings on paper unfold in sequence; they have a specific place on the spatial plane; they are "distinct".

The marks made by a painter exist within a different spectrum. Cézanne's intuitions concerning the void inform his understanding of the plane surface of objects in configuration as well as the plane surface of the canvas. Either the surface or skin is reified into an object of intense interest or worship, or it is seen as no more than a defence against some void conceived of as an absolute disintegration.[2] It was Cézanne's conviction that he had to undergo some experience of the disintegrating void if he were to know how an integration might be arrived at through some reconciliation of different plane surfaces. Arguably, Cézanne's literalist fascination with the plane surface of the picture, and with the presence of the plane surface in the configuration of objects of representation, exists in tandem with another impulse—one that is contrary to it and that cultivates with literalist intensity the intuition that the canvas might be a portal into different dimensions of space.

The canvas is clearly there—it is like a wall—but it also mediates between types of space. The signs "float" into being; and the subject–object relation shifts into the background. Types of space appear, only then to disappear, so that signs might form. Wonder is a counterpart to intuitions concerning these types of space. The translucence of the canvas is comparable as a manifestation of the imaginative to a music in silence.

A way that mind situates itself

Mauss cites a most profound remark of Father Thavenet about the Algonquian notion of *manitou*: "It more particularly designates any being which does not yet have a common name and which is unfamiliar. Of a salamander, a woman said she was afraid: it was a *manitou*. People laughed at her, telling her that its name was a salamander. Trade beads are *manitou*'s scales. Cloth, that wonderful thing, is the skin of a *manitou*". [Lévi-Strauss, 1950: 54]

A hunter, moving through a mist, sees a shape emerge out of the forest. His perception of it is "clear"—he knows something is there. But his perception, although "clear", is in Cartesian terms indistinct: he cannot place the shape within a context, and so he cannot define it.

The criterion for truth to be "clear" and "distinct" depends on the grammar of subject (mind), verb (perceive/evaluate), and object (of possible cognition). It depends on what Lévi-Strauss has described as "a certain way which the mind situates itself in the presence of things. . . ."

> Conceptions of the *mana* [or *manitou*] type are so frequent and so widespread that it is appropriate to wonder whether we are not dealing with a universal and permanent form of thought, which, far from characterising certain civilisations, or archaic or semi-archaic so-called "stages" in the evolution of the human mind, might be a function of a certain way that the mind situates itself in the presence of things, which must therefore make an appearance whenever that mental situation is given. [Lévi-Strauss, 1950: 53]

From a Cartesian perspective, the object of possible cognition is an object that is capable of *endurance,* since it continues to exist within an enduring conception of space and time. A mind that does not see the object in that respect may be thought to be unable to maintain a relation to duration. *Manitou* or *mana* are, then, non-existents. But from another point of view, *manitou* or *mana* indicate an intuition concerning a certain kind of unknowability, which imposes a state of eclipse on the embodied mind—intermittence as an augury of the iconic and of the presence of *existence itself.*

From an ontological and non-Cartesian perspective, *enduring* has no value. Enduring for *existence itself* is an "immaterial" condition, because *existence itself* is unconstrained by duration. Its relation to spatio-temporality is to spatio-temporality as a *multiple* of systems. Within its terms, the notion that there might be one type of spatio-temporal system only, one that is

characterised by an evolution through sequence, is untenable—
except as a blanket denial of the existence of the aniconic.

Saussure detaches his understanding of the structures of
sign system from psychology. He isolates its culture from men-
talist interpretation, as though it were a poetic symbol, or form
of life, emanating from the threshold between *existence itself*
and the schemas of time. Although he raises the issue of zero
function, as clearly a factor in this way of perception, he does
not put pressure on it, or really bring out the value of its
importance.

Lévi-Strauss, in following him, elaborates on the significance of zero in the symbolist structures of myth and conceives
of zero as transforming the basic constituent of myth—which is
discontinuity—into a form of continuity (an empty continuity,
whose meaning, if any, is rhetorical, a gesture of reconciliation).
In Lévi-Strauss's (Cartesian) understanding, zero is often the
factor in a group delusion, which enables the group to continue
operating in seeming amicability; and therefore it is not unlike
the Cartesian phantom limb, which the patient with the amputated leg summons up to make his sense of pain "distinct" as
well as "clear".

In this view, all concepts must emerge from experience:
specifically from mind's engagement, as subject, with an object
that is presumed to be knowable.[3] People who invoke *mana* to
make sense of their perceptions end up with a cipher—at best
usable in diplomatic negotiation between groups—because they
wish to be in touch with some object of possible cognition. It is
not that they might wish to make a link, by way of the contact
barrier, with "O". Lévi-Strauss's Cartesian view is informative
about zero in the semantic of signs. It is not informative about
zero as a potential symbol. It does not describe zero as a function of the aniconic; it therefore does not describe the significance of the iconic.[4]

Ontology, in centring on the unknowable nature of Being
and on the logic in transformation by which the concepts of
Becoming arise from an unknowable source, gives less status
than psychology does to the verifying powers of the sensory
apparatus. It observes how the sensory apparatus, while trans-

acting with states of Becoming, is unable to apprehend states of Being—and that the sensory apparatus has no means of knowing that it is inoperative, when Being has rendered it inoperative. In ontology, the idea of *music in silence* indicates the matrix out of which a certain music might arise. But empirically such an idea is without value, and the sensory apparatus is liable to dismiss it and not to see its significance as a concept of the imagination. It is ontological to think of certain kinds of silence as creative—and also as forms of truth, although the silences are by their nature indistinct. And in the ideology of the imagination, at least, and in ways that I do not understand, silence is a factor in the tempering of noise into sound.

Ontology provides a key to understanding how signs might relate to location. Silence, as a matrix to music, is a "ground" out of which signs emerge. It is comparable to the plane surface of a canvas on which a painter works, which from a certain aspect is a metaphysical portal: the signs are like angels going to and fro on Jacob's ladder. The marks that the painter makes undergo the discontinuity of crossing a threshold; they do not have the continuity of writing, which is maintained by placing the threshold as far away as possible from the writer. In writing, the threshold is the vanishing point in perspective, the *oubliette* through which symbolically the victim of the sacrifice disappears. In painting, the threshold appears to be inseparably an aspect of the wall-like plane surface of the canvas, as though the concept of the canvas surface were some rudimentary intimation of forms of disjunctive transformation in architecture, such as the altar or temple reify.

Notes

1. However, I need a psychologist with ontological intuitions to demonstrate to me why an optic pit might be a source of insight.

2. Esther Bick's theory of "second skin" can be related informatively to this aesthetic.

3. Bion's theory of *preconception* marks an attempt to shore up this theory. The theory of preconception hinges on the existence of some object

of possible cognition, by which it is realised. Preconception is quite different from contact barrier, although phenomenologically, in relation to the *latent*, it may appear similar.

4. In other words, Lévi-Strauss's view on zero is informative about the contact barrier as the enabler of the neutrons as the imaginary twins, but it is not informative about the contact barrier as disjunctive transformer, which activates catastrophic change. And yet Lévi-Strauss provides his readers with concepts that help to explicate the nature of the second meaning of the contact barrier.

8

Inspiration & breakdown

Perturbed by his experience of beauty as an actual event in the world, Socrates in the *Phaedo* feels obliged to turn to an imperceptible realm of forms to find his bearings. But his conception of the imaginative is isolated from the oceanic terrors of drowning. He conceives of it as an archive of texts, to which no reader has access, but in which every reader must have faith—the ultimate storehouse of truth. The inaccessibility of the realms of forms brings it perilously close to the concept of *deus otiosus*.

Arguably, Socrates was less perturbed by some actual event than by his intuiting a poetic symbol, the roots of which lay in the indistinct and inaccessible realm of forms. But he does not describe this symbol in terms of sign language; he describes it as a form of writing, as something that must be locatable. If pain does not arise from event, it must arise from some source that has the status of a location, even though it is inaccessible. This would save it from being thought of as indistinct, like the *mana* of Thavenet's description. Socrates' realm of forms theory is a way of saving the appearance of location, in spite of his intuition that the source of inspiration is always indeterminate, of a celestial light unpacking within light within light, indefinitely—which is one way of describing the idea of grace.

Within reverie, the gaze of the transference, which is grace itself, provides a sense of indefinite distance. A rationality that operates in terms of duration will falter when faced by this type of sign thinking. It is as though the thinker, as the one who in reverie experiences herself or himself as an object of reverie, were to meet on this threshold the two concurrent infinities, as described by the narrator of Plato's *Timaeus*, in which smallness decreases *ad infinitum*, as largeness increases *ad infinitum*. It is not possible to focus on this dual awareness of the infinitely microscopic and the infinitely telescopic, except to say that it would seem to inform the habitual denial that traditional cosmology makes concerning the existence of the concept of magnitude. It is as though the concept of magnitude had to disappear if there were to be revelation by way of the sign.

A psychology without an ontology is unable to describe the role of inspiration in experience. Descartes himself hoped to use the logic of psychology to make a transition into ontology; but he could not work out the foundations to this logic. Mind rejects ego's attempts to impose its own conception of *ratio* on it. Ego then categorises the rejection as "breakdown", on the grounds that it believes itself to be the source of its own reality. However, "breakdown", as Plato envisages it through Socrates' perturbation when encountering the beautiful, is the one means by which psychology is able to intuit (without logic) its basis through some process of disjunction and transformation in ontology.

In the *Phaedo*, and starting from the facts of psychology, Plato demonstrates through Socrates' testimony how certain psychological conditions impel belief in an ontological ground to experience. The disorientating power of passion reflects the disorientating power of an ontological *ratio*. In the *Timaeus*, however, Plato reverses this process, starting with the "facts" of ontology, and by means of traditional cosmology as a theory about making, or creationism, seeks to relate symbolism to instrumentality by describing how a demiurge, as agent for some aniconic unknowable, is able to create within a heavenly "nowhere" the iconic conditions of a symbol.

Conceivably, Socrates and the demiurge are aspects of the same person, who in breakdown, or heartbreak, has a dream in which he, finding himself a demiurge, re-makes the cosmos out of a state of breakdown—as though he, the dreamer, were attempting to make sense of a state of perturbation by locating it in some inaccessible archive of prototypes that the celestial artisan is able to dispatch into the earth's domain as a succession of geometric forms.[1] Socrates responds to breakdown by fashioning icons of thought out of the aniconic, even though he holds to the writing conception.[2]

Inspiration can impel the one who is inspired to seek for a description of the experience in terms of a field that is other than the field of the experience itself. The breakdown that impels some translation of the object of breakdown into an imperceptible prototype, or "form", is analogous to the attempt to clarify understanding of the indistinct by evoking *mana* or its equivalents. In order to define the iconic, one has to assume conditions that are disjunctively detached from the icon, as does Plato's astronomer Timaeus when he invokes the aniconic presence of eternity in order to recognise the iconic nature of time. In other words, although time systems may depend on types of sequence, they do not derive from systems of sequentiality; they derive from a symbolism whose source is non-experiential. Multiple forms of time, as forms of music, arise from some matrix in silence.

An object of possible cognition, the potency of which is overwhelming, is liable to abnegate any evidence of itself as an object in experience and to discover its inheritance in some inaccessible source. Feeling himself to be destroyed by the beauty of Laura, whom he no more than glimpses before losing any sight of her, Petrarch discovers his vocation as a poet, and he is saved from despair by the sight of an actual pool that is so deep that even to this day its depth has not been ascertained.

Socrates' archive and Petrarch's pool are symbols for the imaginative, of varying degrees of effectiveness. Which is logically prior: the meeting with Laura, or the sight of the pool? Conceivably, the pool as icon, or poetic symbol of an aniconic depth, is the means of containment that allows Petrarch to find words for the pain that Laura has aroused, in the same way as an angelic, even though non-existent, Cartesian limb gives meaning to a pain that is otherwise senseless.

A poetic symbol translates out of Becoming into Being and then returns in the form of *yantras*, or sacred geometric forms, as images for the inwardness of form in thought; and the becoming of "O" presents itself an alternative to the subject–object distinction.

Implicit in this type of thinking is a model of the sacrifice. The sacrificer *is* the sacrificed in the act of the sacrifice, no matter where the sacrifice might be situated. Socrates, as someone capable of undergoing actual experiences, is by this submission to sacrifice able to move from psychology into ontology, while Socrates, as the demiurge–artisan, "sacrifices" the soul essences out of which he makes his art-work—consider the "living" clay in the hands of the potter—and creates objects that are meaningful within the psychology of perception. Socrates' refusal in the *Phaedo* to communicate his thoughts about his experience of beauty—he keeps silent—enacts the indeterminacy, symbolised by silence, of any journey from a psychology founded in ontology into an ontology without psychology (Becoming into Being). Conversely, the demiurge's transformation in the *Timaeus* of an ontological situation by means of icon-making (Being into Becoming) entails a translation through the indeterminate transition of a disjunction in transformation. However, *anima mundi* or universal soul-stuff—part of which the demiurge offers up in sacrifice, and with which he is identified—is a surrogate for a pain which is like a dismemberment.

Notes

1. As though they were spiralling snowflakes? The Dogon describe a similar concept of entering the earth's atmosphere in terms of uncoiling spirals and watery meanders (see chapter 21). The linking of spiralling snowflakes to the imagination is Coleridgean.

2. The emporiumuu that destroys the stereotypes of thinking on which Socrates routinely depends also activates a dimension in his dreaming, as a form of life that continues, whether he is asleep or awake.

9

Metaphysical space: "The argument compels us to bring to light, and to describe, a form that is difficult and obscure"

There are "three distinct realities before the world came into existence: Being, space and Becoming".

Plato, *Timaeus,* 52

The discovery of representation. That representation might arise out of an existence that has no need for representation, *existence itself*, suggests that the object of representation might be "that which is discovered" rather than "that which is given". Representation is not a matter of fact, nor is it an essential building block in metaphysics. Contrary to the empiricist's view, it might even be an exceptional fact in the universe. It is the transforming presence of "O", rather than the presence of the subject–object model, that generates the discovery of representation in its fragility—as though all representation were like the falling of snowflakes. By means of multiple spatio-temporal schemas, "O" appears out of the indeterminate.

There is a similarity between the distinction that the narrator in Plato's *Timaeus* draws between Being and Becoming and the distinction that Spinoza draws between *existence itself* and types of existence dependent on spatio-temporal schemas. If there is a difference between these distinctions, it lies in a conception of metaphysical space as an attribute of Being, which Plato's narrator has, and indeed discovers, and which does not appear to interest Spinoza.

> By recognizing Space as an independent and eternally exist-ing factor necessary to the becoming of a world of sensible images, Plato has added to a scheme borrowed from Parmenides. . . . Space is "everlastingly existent: it does not admit of destruction". Time is a work of intelligence and it has an archetype. But Space is without an archetype. [Cornford, 1937: 193][1]

Plato's concept of metaphysical space is a major discovery, like Spinoza's concept of *existence itself*. And yet neither thinker thought fit to enlarge on the meaning of their discoveries, per-haps because they had raised concepts so vast in implication that they could be unseen to those who had thought them, even though they were, as ideas, continuously present to them.

Plato's narrator assumes that the metaphysical dynamic by which Being generates the objects of Becoming depends, for its basis in transformation, on the hypothesis of an extensibility that is a variable. Unlike the types of space that the senses register, metaphysical space is either too sensitive, or too fast, or too slow for intuition to grasp it. Myth frequently locates it in some unknowable optic: in the air and fire (or darkness) of the heavens, and in the ocean's depths. It is unlike the ground on which a text might form. Related to it are sensations concerning the indefinite and the indistinct, which occur within the penum-bra of annihilation. In an equivocal fashion, it threatens cata-strophic change. The poetic symbol comes into existence in conditions that are random.

Plato's narrator relates metaphysical space to receptacles of transformation, which conveniently might be called cosmo-grams.[2] This would link metaphysical space and ontological transformation to an idea of enclosure. But such a linking would appear to have intimidated Pluto, who draws back, sensing (I would think) that if he should discover the random to be mean-ingful, he would undermine any understanding that he might have of rationality. The cosmograms that his narrator describes are either disturbing (as represented by the shaking of a winnowing basket) or overtly related to delusion (the hysterical womb in the *Timaeus*, or the cave of deceptive fire images in the *Republic*).

Metaphysical space is a field of force. If *yantras* or mandalas are charismatic as sacred spaces, they are so because they are translations of the aesthetic of the field of force into the structures of form. Judeo-Christian theologians, from a different position, define metaphysical space as conditioned by the vagaries of the Holy Spirit, while thinkers in many religious denominations have defined it as the environment of prayer. Breuer and Freud deny this space its metaphysical significance (but not entirely) when they define it as transference and as the settings in which transference occurs.

Metaphysical space is the threshold space of ontological transformation. As the fundamental space of transferential phenomena, it indicates how Freud's concept of contact barrier invokes within the transference a transformation by means of the indistinct. It is the space that Mauss thought of as *mana* and Lévi-Strauss redefined in terms of zero. Many cultures and rituals would place this floating signifier within some almost imperceptible conception of a threshold or boundary or frontier, which contains and possibly anodises the indefinite. The contact barrier may seem to be neutral and enabling, but this is only one of its aspects.

Notes

The quotation in the chapter title is from Plato, *Timaeus,* 49.

1. Space, as "everlastingly existent" and as not admitting of destruction, is space as a contact-barrier enabler. This is one definition of metaphysical space. But metaphysical space also has the significance of being a means of purification by way of destruction, the forge as eye of the sun through which the holy ones are able to walk.

2. The concept of cosmogram revises the concept of microcosm in that it presumes that any basic constituent of the cosmos, such as it is, enacts the dynamic of sacrifice and creation in the now of every moment.

10

The organs of divine intelligence

Pythagoras' description of the mystery of creation in terms of an *auditory* perspective occurs at an earlier period in time than Plato's *visual* perspective on the mystery of creation.

He was once engaged in intense thought about whether he could find some precise scientific instrument to assist the sense of hearing, as compass and ruler and the measurement of angles assist the sight and scales and weights and measures assist touch. Providentially, he walked passed a smithy, and heard the hammers beating out the iron on the anvil. They gave out a melody of sounds, harmonious except for one pair. He recognized in them the consonance of octave, fifth and fourth, and saw that what lay between the fourth and fifth was in itself discordant, but that it was essential in filling out the greater of the intervals. Rejoicing in the thought that the gods were helping on his project [i.e. *the music in silence*—my interpolation], he ran into the smithy, and discovered by detailed experiments that the difference of sound was in relation to the weight of the hammers, not the force used by those hammering, the shape of the hammer heads, or any change in the iron as it was beaten out. [Iamblichus, in Clark, 1989: 50–51]

The quality of Pythagoras' talent in listening to the clashing of hammers in a smithy suggests that he was able to enter into an identification with the music in silence of planetary movement. In Dogon creationism the power of the Word, at its third appearance, is able to lower to earth a smithy that exists in the heavens. Pythagoras' relation to the Word, on the contrary, would seem to have had him release a terrestrial forge from its terrestrial tethering, so that it is able to rise up into the stars.[1]

While terrestrial hearing and utterance are related to fire and noise, the occurrence of heavenly hearing and utterance within the metaphysical space of the heavens has to be translated into silence and light if it is to be recognised. Divine intelligence deteriorates as it descends. Meteors falling over the deserts of ancient Egypt fragmented or disappeared into fire as they entered the atmosphere, as though they were gods too virtuous for earthly living. Blacksmiths and their assistants would pick up bits of left-over twisted meteor metal and turn them into adzes, which priests would then use to break open the clamped mouths of corpses, so that the souls of the dead could escape like soul-birds into the sky (Wainwright, 1932).

By means of the matrix of silence, Pythagoras, as shaman– demiurge, is able to reconstitute the destroyed poetic symbol; he intuits in dissonance the temperings of sound, which form into the geometry of music. He has the creativity of a blacksmith-god.

Through some unutterable, almost inconceivable likeness to the gods, his hearing and his mind were intent upon the celestial harmonies of the cosmos. It seemed as if he alone could hear and understand the universal harmony and music of the spheres and of the stars which move within them, uttering a song more complete and satisfying than any human melody, composed of subtly varied sounds of motion and speeds and sizes and positions, organized in a logical and harmonious relation to each other, and achieving a melodious circuit of subtle and exceptional beauty. [Iamblichus, in Clark, 1989: 27]

At a later period in time, Philo conjectured that the ideas of Plato were thoughts in the mind of God. Pythagoras concretely lives out a similar conjecture concerning the divinisation of thought. From debris, he construes the idea of the forms that constitute the music of the spheres. The absence that disappears with the emerging of the music contains within itself a sense of expectation, which the music articulates and to which it gives form. Realising the expectation is a function of awe.

Notes

1. An analogue for this kind of thinking, in terms of the *yantra*, would be an idea of the mandala ground-plan as transforming into an architectural presence—the stupa as the very presence of divine being.

11

Body as an intermediary for existence itself

> Eternal and uncreated, Amma is the sky, and his Word
> represents the air among the four elements. The Word is
> his before all creation. He forms and fertilises the
> original placenta by it. The Word is "within"; as a
> thought which is unformulated, but it invents the
> physical matter which gives form to thought.
>
> Calame-Griaule, 1965: 94

In the legend of Pythagoras and the smithy, the meta-physical space of sky—which in a sense is a no-place, be-cause Pythagoras' contemporaries had no access to it—is able to transform noise into auditory–visual patternings of a tempered kind. The sky purges noise in the same way as the fire in the forge purges metals. The sonority in stillness of music is the silence in movement of the constellations: this is one of the meanings of the "music of the spheres". Metaphysical space as a transformer is the site of the sacrifice which, when brought to earth, reveals itself to be the interior of a holy sepulchre, in which a body disappears as a function of its being tempered into some undying form.

The noise emitted by the Pythagorean smithy, when purified by the silence of the sky, transfigures into music. Transference, similarly, is an articulation of silence, which requires neither ears nor mouth, and which tempers noise into sound. On this level of thinking, the terrestrial and the celestial smithy are the same place.

In sign systems, the source of signs is without location. To relate the source to the vicissitudes of birth (the past) or to the vicissitudes of death (the future) is to marginalise its significance. The sacrifice occurs in the timelessness of the now. Out of the body as nothing, there arises the idea of a link without subject and object, transference as a form of prayer. Breathing, hearing, and seeing arise from the body. In the myth of Adam's sacrifice, the rib extracted from Adam's body is a link without subject or object, which transfigures into the presence of grace—Eve as transfiguring the dead Adam into a breathing or a sighing.

In the logic of traditional cosmology, a body is an art-work created through an act of destruction, an icon created by way of an act of dismemberment. The plenitude of the cosmos depends on some act of absolute negation. The breathing or sighing of an absence, where a body once was, are emanations that mark the beginning of a transformation. By way of links without subject and object, the sign system reforms itself. "Breathing" and "sighing", as occurring within the space of the threshold, are links that do not attach to subject and object.[1]

Bruce Lincoln has observed that the Vedic text of the *Aitareya Upanishad* describes microcosm and macrocosm as alternating in a kind of "breathing" and compares the breathing of the microcosm to the sound of a macrocosm, which is like a high wind.

> Whenever the cosmos is created, the body is destroyed and— conversely—whenever the body is created, the cosmos is destroyed. . . . As one exhales, breath leaves the body through the nose and enters the wind, leaving the wind and rejoining the body upon inhalation. The simple act of breathing thus alternately constructs the macrocosm (while deconstructing

the microcosm), then constructs the microcosm (while deconstructing the macrocosm). [Lincoln, 1986: 33–35]

But parts of the body also give issue to other faculties, like "hearing", which grammatically is a gerund that can exist without subject and object.

> Similarly, as sound travels into the distance and ceases to be heard, the cardinal directions (the utmost statement of spatial distance) come into being as the sound enters them, while the ears fall apart, being no longer in use. But when sound travels from the distance and is heard by the ears, distance ceases to be, and the ears are reconstituted through the act of hearing. [Lincoln, 1986: 33–35]

In a process of alternation, ears or hearing become the quarters of the cosmos, or the quarters of the cosmos become ears/hearing. The relation of these gerund-like links to the model of part and whole, is one in which parts of a dismembered body become types of sound, possibly in the same way as parts of certain (visual) mandalas become the utterance of mantras (Tucci, 1949: 94). Thus the words that make up a specific type of stanza in Vedic poetry, or the parts of a dismembered sacrificial body, or the taking apart and the putting together of bricks in the altar, are analogues for each other.

> The body of Prajâpati, who is the sacrifice, is composed of the gods who, if they did not go so far as to abolish themselves in him, at least allowed themselves to be "eaten" by him. . . . The altar of bricks is more than the mere copy of that altar which would originally have constituted Prajâpati's real body. Already in the myth, we find an account of the transmutation by which Fire on the one hand, and the elements of time on the other, were first materialized into bricks. . . .
> Each of the different parts of the body of this Prajâpati-Agni-Soma (his head, neck, spinal column, wings, knees, etc.) is the seat of a divinity in the pantheon, but also—and this is fundamental—of an element of the Veda. More exactly, it is a matrix for one of the metric schemata operative in Vedic

poetry. So, for example, the abdomen is the place reserved for the god Indra, and is also the place reserved for a specific stanza of four verses of eleven syllables each. [Malamoud, 1989: 217]

In inspiration occurs the beginnings of the transformation by which the cosmos in negation becomes the cosmos in plenitude. There is a breathing or sighing, in which "no one" breathes or sighs and "no one" hears the breathing or sighing.

1. The acts of "breathing" and of "sighing" are similar to the writing that, certain of the Gourmantché believe, appears spontaneously on the skin of the victim of the sacrifice. They are "forms of life", arising out of "nowhere", like the poetic symbol. There is an absence of bodily organs as either the subject or the object of the link.

2. The body of the victim, equated with the cosmos itself, is everything or nothing. Its coming into existence marks the evolution of duration, including the "distances" in intimacy that define human relationships. Janus-headed "fusions" between father and son, or between mother and son, as prototypes of murder and incest, lie embedded within the presence of the sacred king.

3. Cosmograms manifest the emergence of a specific type of time as an icon for *existence itself*. The body of the victim of the sacrifice exists in a space in which temporal schemas are in the process of emerging.

Myths demonstrate that the Word can manifest itself as a type of link that does not have to be related to specific subjects or objects and as the form of reversible structure, in which the aniconic enters into the forms of duration known as the event. Icons, as a consequence of sign-system thinking, cannot be accounted for in terms of theories of duration. They cannot be verified or justified. They shadow forth the beginnings of a place and time. In Cartesian terms, they are *almost* "distinct", in spite of being "clear". They describe *acts of making* that resemble prayer, creations of the Holy Spirit, although supernatural figures like the demiurge may seem to control the process of making.

Note

1. From another aspect, the transformations of the sacrifice are thought to be "contained" by the primal scene, or to appear as "writing" on the walls of the temple, or on the skin of the victim of the sacrifice.

12

Discovery & revelation

If a dead person could think, the dead person might hold
to the belief that *everything is in the state of having been
given.* A criterion for being alive is that this definition is
untenable. For a living person, nothing is given; and everything
is related either to discovery or to revelation. A functionalist is
someone who thinks in terms of discovery: everything is in the
process of being discovered. A symbolist is someone who thinks
that everything is revelation—and that only some non-existent
king beneath the water, or some imaginary demiurge who lives
on the threshold, has the privilege of making discoveries.

For the functionalist, the phenomenon of transference is
comparable to a shuttle (or contact barrier) by which the dyad of
subject and object weaves meanings. For the symbolist, transference is a poetic symbol, which arises out of the indeterminacy
of a metaphysical space in which the contact barrier is the
becoming of "O". To move from a functionalist conception of the
contact barrier to a symbolist conception entails some sort of
leap. For the functionalist, the mathematics of the dyad in
transference is that one and one equals two; and that the contact barrier as the dyad's shuttle makes the elements equal

three. For the symbolist, the model is one that the theologians of the Trinity have long perceived, in which three is one and one is three. The instability of this model, its asymmetry, is induced by the indeterminacy, or source in grace, of a cosmos founded in a process of creation and uncreation.

For the functionalist the discovery of transference is as momentous as the discovery of electricity. Either member of the dyad might wish to control this potency and to make use of it, often with different motives. For the symbolist, *existence itself*, as the "something other", generates acts of creation, which occur on some threshold associated with metaphysical space. Revelation, as arising from the music of silence, from silence as a matrix, results from the *vibrancy* of this transformation, as it crosses the metaphysical space of the threshold into the domain of spatio-temporal schemas. There are no means to measure the spatio-temporal conditions of the journey.

In many, if not most, religions, prayer and sacrifice are inseparable elements—indeed, the bedrock to religious aspiration *is* prayer and sacrifice. Transference, as secular prayer, is an emanation from the void. As sacrifice, it is the means that contracts subject and object into each other, sacrificer and sacrificed, a time-arresting fusion, as in the image of the father–son Janus-headed figure. Freud would seem to have intuited the link of sacrifice and prayer when he centred psychoanalysis on the sacrifice myth of Oedipus. Sacrifice is the agony that acts of prayer modify.

The Cartesian seeks for a poetic symbol to underpin the unstable relationships of mind and body and self and other. But the symbol sought—Descartes's God—is, in effect, the source of the instability, since the theology of *three in one and one in three* cannot be squared with the functionalist assumption of *one plus one equals two*. Contact barrier as enabler, contact barrier as Descartes's compliant God, as that which supports the dyad, however incompatible the elements of the dyad might be, has to yield to the idea of contact barrier as disjunctive transformer, as the catastrophic means of the becoming of "O".

In Cartesianism, the poetic symbol exists outside the culture of mind and body. It has to "prove" its existence. It has to find some way into the culture of mind and body. The ancient Greek theory of the *symbolon* also depends on a denial of catastrophic change, as does Aristotle's dismissal of the *music-of-the-spheres* theory, as part of his aim to deny validity to Plato's theory of ideas.

The *symbolon* theory describes the coming together of two elements, which are fragments of a lost integration. The meaning of the gap between the two elements depends on its being a gap that can be decreased. In the theory of contact barrier as "O", the dyad disappears into contact barrier as the catastrophic transforming power of the poetic symbol. In the theory of the *symbolon*, the contact barrier as means of linkage disappears into the combining of the dyad. Freud's first description of the contact barrier is implicitly a *symbolon* theory; it limits the contact barrier to being a system of negotiation.

> In classical Greek, *symbolon* was at first related to a "drawing together". In a meeting or party the symbols could be contributions to a shared meal. In the control mechanisms of a contract, the two parts of a token, which were to be separated by the contracting parties and brought together again, were called *symbola* and had the function of tallies. In both cases there is an element of contrast (there are at least two "partners" in a party or contract) and an element of likeness (the "partners" share a purpose or the "parts" fit together). Thus even the earliest terminology implied that the symbol is different in some ways from that which it represents and nevertheless similar or even one with it. [Ladner, 1979: 239–240]

> *Symbolon* is "password, formula of belief, and sacrament in the non-Christian mystery cults of antiquity". [ibid.: n4]

Aristotle pivots his *Poetics* on a similar notion of recognition, and on the kind of metaphor thinking, in which one form of knowable is discovered to be related to another form of knowable. He assumes, controversially, that the poetic symbol might be related to re-cognition rather than to some state of unknowing, in which cognition, as an idea, loses authority. In recognition, a nurse is able to link her perception of a scar on Ulysses' body to her recollection of the scar that she had seen on the body of Ulysses as a child. The excitement of discovery provides a retroactive status to the neatness of the act of fitting together.

But recognition, as the fitting together of tallies, operates on the level of code-breaking; it idealises the unsubstantiated authority of memory. Fundamentally, it depends on the psychology of crowd thinking and on states of anomie. The stranger in the crowd turns out to be some long-lost friend: within such states, the idea of transference as symbol is limited to being a theory of transference as function. "Like" discovers "like"; and the imaginative, which can be inexplicable and seldom entails acts of re-finding, is the serrated edge that disappears when the symbolon tallies are united.

The subject, in listening to the object, presumes that the act of listening is the key with which the subject is able to open the door to knowledge about the object. At the end of his life Freud opposed such an understanding. States of psychic extension (intuition?) might be more aptly associated with states of "un-knowing", a mysterious unburdening of knowledge. As "O", the poetic symbol increases states of learned ignorance.

The metaphysical space out of which revelation arises, and which Plato distrusts even though he is able to intuit it, cannot be approached by the type of intuition that operates by means of verbs of cognition. Aristotle thinks to know all that needs to be known about the imperceptible domain of ideas, or of the music of the spheres, in part because he denies the existence of some indeterminate metaphysical space in which psychic extensions related to unknowing might occur. By thinking of cognitive verbs as functions, he can consider himself the arbiter of their meanings. He appropriates to himself the role of demiurge in thinking himself to be the verb, or act, that unites one tally with the other. Wishing away the existence of the poetic symbol puts revelation outside the precincts of functionalism.

Augustine spent twelve years in trying to sort out the significance of the logic of three in one and one in three. The gravity of the problem remains, in spite of Augustine's belief that he had failed to make much headway with it. It is present in any sensation of "the other", as a potent if inaccessible presence. Recent discoveries in relation to the nature of concrete thinking, and in relation to the role of the floating signifier in mythic structure, have been informative about the nature of the difficulties that confronted Augustine.

13

"The divine artificers make receptacles in order to create time"

The name of the scarab-beetle-god Khepri means "becoming", and in the mythology of the ancient Egyptians this small creature must carry the significance of all objects of Becoming. The luminous dawn kingdom behind the horizon known as the *akhet*, over which Khepri presides, is a prototype for Plato's imperceptible metaphysical space—the ground that enables Being to initiate the objects of Becoming. A frequent emblem on ancient Egyptian coffins shows a scarab beetle's head with the red circle of the sun raised above it. Khepri sets in motion the beginning of the sun-god Re's daily journey over the eastern horizon. But at the moment when time, or Becoming, originates, Khepri has to disappear (sacrificed?), in order that Re might be born.[1]

First light, whose source, if any, is concealed, represents visually the originating of duration. It is an analogue for the imperceptible sound of heavenly night music, by which Pythagoras is able to intuit the idea of harmony in form, while listening to the dissonance that arises out of the fire of a forge. First light is the contact-barrier space in which one twin is born and the other twin dies; it is a zero variable.

The sun, when it goes down, does not die but reaches the hidden fountain of its life. Becoming or arising is the nature of Khepri. His name makes that plain. But every arising occurs in and from death, which thus appears to be potential life. In the spot where Khepri dies—on the western horizon—his nature as the god of resurrection is realized, and this is why he must have his dwelling there. When in the morning he steps out of his dwelling the mystery of his revival is already accomplished. Darkness is the cradle of light; in it the sun finds the power to arise. *The land of life* is a frequent name for the nocturnal abode of the sun. Absolute life has its home in the realm of death. [Rambova, 1957: 30, quoting W. B. Kristensen]

First light is the indeterminate or metaphysical space out of which a circle, in appearing, diverges into the two circles of sacrifice and divination, as some of the Gourmantché conceive of it. Bits of the sacral body disappear into the circle of the sacrifice (the culture of Khepri) and reappear by way of the other circle as signs of divination (the rays of the ascending sun). The kingdom of first light behind the horizon, although indistinct, marks the transformation by which *existence itself* puts the body of time to the sacrifice, so that it might be translated into the symbolism of time as icon of eternity.

In ancient Egypt the world becomes light at dawn long before sunrise, and it is almost full daylight before the sun comes up over the horizon. Equally it is still light when the sun is obscured by clouds . . . that light is one thing and the sun is another thing finds its expression in the story of the Creation. In Genesis i, 3–5, it is said that God created the light and divided the light from the darkness, calling the one Day and the other Night. This was the first day. It was not until the fourth day that "God said, Let there be lights in the firmament of the heaven", which were the stars and "two great lights; the greater light to rule the day, and the lesser light to rule the night" (Gen. i, 14–16).

Even as late as the writing of Genesis, the sun, moon, and stars were only part and parcel of the sky, and light was still thought to exist without them. [Wainwright, 1938: 94–95]

Iconic markers of time.   A legend in the third-century writings of St Nilus (Robertson Smith, 1894) specified that first light was the time in which the desert people had to practise the rites of sacrifice. The rites had to be completed, and all evidence of the sacrificed body had to disappear, before the rays of the sun appeared over the horizon.

> The camel chosen as the victim is bound upon a rude altar of stone piled together, and when the leader of the band has thrice led the worshippers around the altar in a solemn procession accompanied with chants, he inflicts the first wound while the last words of the hymn are still upon the lips of the congregation, and in all haste drinks of the blood that gushes forth. Forthwith the whole company fall on the victim with their swords, hacking off bits of the quivering flesh and devouring them raw with such wild haste, that in the short interval between the rise of the day star which marked the hour for the service to begin, and the disappearance of its rays before the rising sun, the entire camel, body and bones, skin, blood and entrails is wholly devoured. The plain meaning of this is that the victim was devoured before its life had left the still warm blood and flesh—raw flesh is called "living" flesh in Hebrew and Syriac—and that thus in the most literal way all those who shared in the ceremony absorbed part of the victim's life into themselves. [Robertson Smith, 1894: 338]

The body submitted to the sacrifice and the place of the sacrifice are an actual body and an actual place. But they are also aspects of the cosmos as a symbol, which is in a continuous process in the *now* of being contracted and rarefied, eclipsed and freed from eclipse. The body in sacrifice, as *nothing and everything,* is indistinguishably the cosmos as light and darkness, water and sky, order and chaos. The sun appears out of the act of sacrifice. Disposing of the camel's body entirely—by eating, as well as presumably by other means, since no one can eat bones—must have entailed magical practices.[2]

   Location and translocation are "indistinct" themes within the ontological transformations of the becoming of "Ω". The solar presence, rising over the edge of the horizon, originates temporal markings within an indefinite space: it operates from beyond the life-and-death space–time exigencies of the spectator.[3] Leaping flames (as in the shrine or in the forge) can represent the inconstancy of its environment. The sacral body, whether animal or luminary, terrestrial or celestial, has many meanings: it is the "body" of the temple, the kingdom, and of the incorporation of the people of the kingdom, as well as the body of the sacred king. It alternates with the void. One circle reveals its guise as the other circle. Signs of the sun-god emerge, as the first *iconic* markers of time. The heavenly and imperceptible body of Khepri is an analogue for the perceptible and terrestrial body of the camel.

Frobenius (in Haberland, 1973: 62–63) has described a central African ceremony of the utmost secrecy, in which, *during the time of first light*, pygmy hunters would draw a sacred circle on the ground.[4] The circle created an image of the future in the present. In the circle, the hunters would draw an image of the animal that they wished to hunt down. They would stick an arrow into the image.[5] The future, as metaphysical space, enters into the present. It is as though the *thought* of the animal, and then its existence as actuality, had to be dragged out of *existence itself*, as an aspect of the iconic. If the hunters managed to kill an animal, they would mix some of its blood, feathers, or skin with earth from the sacred circle and place it within the circle. The first light of yet another day was the time for performing this second series of rites.

Maupoil (1943: 186 et seq.) and Frobenius (in Haberland, 1973), separately, have pointed out that tablets of divination have to be kept out of the full sun, so that they should not fade. A symbolic rather than a functional reason for the seclusion of the tablets is that they are emblems of first light. As symbols of the pre-durational, they must not be used as markers of the temporal.

A shadow in movement can initiate wonder and dread—it can stimulate intuitions concerning temporality. The calligraphy of the shadow, as much as the glare of the sun, has to be avoided. A shadow in movement, or the slow dripping of water, or the burning of a candle are either possible functions, which are sufficient in themselves and for themselves, or they are symbols for the unknowable. But the wonder of time as sequence has a way of abnegating the wonder aroused by the emerging of proportion out of the void. Time as sequence can assume, perhaps absurdly, the authority of being its own cause.

Notes

The quotation in the chapter title is from Kramrisch, 1981: 47–48.

1. In Vedic creationism Indra drives his peg into a dragon sheltered in Varuna's stone house within the primordial mound. By this act, Indra stabilises the mound and releases the sun from its solar stable. The dragon who dies and the sun that rises are the same figure. By analogy the solar dragon is Khepri; and by an even more remote analogy, it is the fire within the Pythagorean forge whose sparks transform into the stars.

2. How did the bones disappear? In the cultures of Hinduism or Buddhism they might have been placed in shrines as relics, as a stage in the dynamics of transformation.

3. "An increasing preoccupation with the relationship of the image to its prototype (rather than to its beholder) and an increasingly strong belief in the potentialities of the image as a vehicle of divine power" (Kitzinger, 1954: 149).

4. *Imenty*, that which is concealed or secret, is primarily a term for the Western lands of the dead among the ancient Egyptians. But within eternity, east and west are aspects of the same hidden divine spirit. The lands of the dead are cognates with the realm of first light and with the immense powers mobilised by a minute creature, the scarab beetle.

5. The *Satapatha-Brâhmana* (in Eggeling, 1894, 2: 175) describes how a Brahmin must drive eleven stakes into the ground of the sacrifice in order to appropriate the earth as sacred space. The stakes are associated to the thunderbolt and to the post to which the object of the sacrifice must be tethered.

14

The incompatibility of prayer & event

> Western tradition has always considered the text as
> being like the physical body—in some way exterior to
> mind, breath, the word, *logos*.
>
> Derrida, 1967: 52

The theologians of Byzantium looked to creationist myths in Genesis and the *Timaeus* to describe how icons formed (Ladner, 1953). In God's extraction of Adam's rib in Genesis, likeness derives from a gap in transformation, or disjunctive transformation, by which a rib metamorphoses into the presence of Eve. Within the garden, and often problematically, the symbol exists in the form of angels and sacred trees. But there is no key to the symbol; and Adam feels secluded because of this absence—in spite of his intimate relationship with God. Being granted the right to name the animals does not give him the key: he requires something other, the act of sacrifice by which God extracts the rib (or *axis mundi*) from his body and releases the presence of grace in the form of Eve. Grace, as the key to the poetic symbol, is random; it does not observe the logic of duration and location; as an intermediary between *existence*

61

itself and duration,[1] it is comparable as a sign language in formation to a gaze *that is synonymous with a certain type of hearing*—a gaze as a listening and uttering that cannot be controlled, a prototype of the feeding object that comes and goes. Grace arises from the sacrifice and yet mutates from it.

Mary Magdalene, as the sexual aspect of the mother who procreates the second Adam, differs from her aspect as the mother who is able to "hear" the voice of the archangel by way of a *gaze*. When Mary Magdalene first sees Christ in relation to the condition of the holy sepulchre as a magical and *emptied* void, she asks him confusedly: *Are you the gardener?*—meaning, are you Adam in relation to myself, as Eve in my sexual aspect? She recognises Christ in his ancestral role as Adam, the first victim: her candour about sexuality is bound up with her respect for the past. But only the other Mary—in her deliberate isolation from the idea of historical knowledge, in her ontological purity—is able to recognise the resurrected Christ as poetic symbol, in the same way as she is able to understand the meaning of the future in the intimation of an archangel's silent utterance.

Icon does not link known to known, as metaphor does. The nature of the iconic likeness of man and God, or time and eternity, is imperceptible. Freud thought of the psyche as not knowing about its state of extension into space. Adam and Oedipus did not know their natural origins—Adam because he had none, Oedipus because his nurturers had deliberately obscured this knowledge. Are these demi-gods prototypes of iconic intuition because they were born into "unknowing"? This is to think by way of the sign language of traditional cosmology, in which the sign, located "out there", arises out of "nowhere". Socratic man recognises this insight and yet somewhat denies it, by turning to the knowability of the writing conception.

An Egyptian priest informs Solon that although the first Athens to be built was destroyed, it still continues to exist, in the form of documents, in the secluded archives of ancient Egypt (*Timaeus*, 21 et seq.). We do not know whether this information had been translated into the mysterious grammar of hieroglyphs. All we know is that the sacrality of Athens depends on its being identified with the cosmic cycles of destruction and regeneration. Socratic man compromises this sign-system belief by attempting to make cosmology distinct, by locating it in the text; but he compromises it in part only. By proposing that the texts are inaccessible, he returns to the source in unknowability, which is the core to sign-system thinking.

By its inaccessibility, the archive of texts reveals itself to be a historical counterpart to the ontological realm of forms, which is also inaccessible. The texts and the ontological forms have the appearance of writing—they are sequential; they are like events—but fundamentally they have the formative structuring of signs. Socratic man is beguiled by the idea that the act of writing should create a temporality of a linear sort, in which it is possible to conjecture that a new entity exists, *the object in history*, in which history is an embalming fluid that preserves the object against ontological supposition. Although the unfolding of a text can be as mysterious and iconic in realisation as the pulse of passing time itself, its sequentiality does lend itself to a denial of the aniconic.

The concurrent destruction and renewal of Plato's Athens, like Virgil's Troy later, guarantees that these cities are equated with the cosmos. Iconic likeness is a "likeness" that contracts into nothing or expands into the totality; in contraction, it is the sacrificer as the sacrificed; in expansion, it is grace, as a third element in the Trinity, that is able to separate father and son out of a Janus-headed figure. By way of an act of sacrifice, the *Timaeus* demiurge is able to take geometric shapes and interpret them as forms of time, much as in the Pythagorean ethos the indeterminate *space* of heavenly bodies in movement can alternate into *time* as the inaudible pulse of the stars.

The equation of microcosm and macrocosm in traditional cosmology lends support to the belief that there is only one narrative and one philosophy.[2] In ancient Egypt one of the smallest forms of life, a deified scarab-beetle, has the power to generate Becoming from the immeasurable. Leibniz, who held to the idea of a *philosophia perennis*, assumed that every form of life, however minimal, was identical with some imaginative conception of the totality.

A rational and male-centred description of the equating of microcosm and macrocosm might indicate that the intermediary, the priest who is sacrificer–sacrificed, is not a scarab-beetle but a Renaissance prince: being someone, in the representations of Vitruvius and Leonardo, who supinely has arms and legs stretched out to the orients. A vertical line, marking *nadir : zenith*, extends upwards and downwards from this "centre" by way of the figure's navel. The orients, to which the arms and legs of the figure extend, gather in many properties of the cosmos, usually categorised in groups of four: the winds, the colours, the idea of four grandparents or of four grandchildren, and so on. In myths from many sources in the world, first man is presented as such a "centre".

> The Zuñis arrange the world into quarters, or rather into several worlds corresponding to the four quarters, the zenith and the nadir. They group towns, wards and totems according to mythic division; and by it they systemise ceremony and government. Each region is given an appropriate colour and number. The north is yellow, because the winter light at morning and evening is yellow, and so is the light of the aurora. The west is the blue world, because twilight is blue or grey twilight at evening, and also because the blue Pacific lies westward from Zuñiland. The south is red, because it is the region of summer and of fire; and the east is white because of the quality of first light. The upper region is many-coloured, like sunlight on the clouds, and the lower region black, like caves and deep sources of water. As the navel of the world, the midmost has all these colours: it contains all the quarters. Each region is the home of a special element: the north is the home of wind, breath, or air, the west of water, the south of fire, and the east of earth and the seeds of earth; correspondingly, the north is the home of winter, the west of spring, the south of summer, and the east of autumn. The Zuñi perform no ceremonial and hold no council, without having a firm view on which position each member of a clan shall occupy, for according to the season, one or another of the clan groups will take precedence. To such an extent, indeed, is the tendency to classify according to the regions that each clan is subdivided according to a six-fold arrangement and according to the subsidiary relations of the six parts of its totem. The notion of the "middle" is central to Zuñi organisation: it has served to give solidarity to the Zuñi

people at the time of its division into separate tribes.
[Cushing, 1896: 367–373]

The system of orientation depends on what Cushing calls the "midmost", or the "navel of the world", or the "navel of mother earth". But the idea of "midmost" is one that can be used to deny the threat of earthquakes. "Earthquakes made the conception of the middle prominent. It was thought that earthquakes would cease, if one could get to the navel of the earth mother" (ibid.). But implicitly midmost and earthquake, centrality and catastrophic change, are linked.

* * *

The body of the victim in the circularity of negation–plenitude is always the body of Adam or of other divine kings. The *philosophia perennis* describes an Adam who is like a great river with many tributaries. In the mythologies of West Africa, Adam is blacksmith, musician (*blacksmith as musician*) and priest–king, as well as the first gardener–agriculturist.[3] His body is a void, out of which a poetic symbol takes on being.

The Genesis and the *Timaeus* creationist myths postulate that all formation is measure. They operate with fixed counters of thought. They are less about beginnings than about renewals. They describe recurrent attempts, by way of the sacrifice, to redeem the profane and broken—the elements as "vestiges", which Plato's narrator thinks of as vestigial because they are godless.

A myth founded on sign-system thinking, the ancient Egyptian myth of Shu (in the Coffin texts [Faulkner, 1973], numbers 75 et seq.), shows how far the bias of the iconism in Genesis and the *Timaeus* is towards the writing mode.[4] The myth describes a rite. A first-born son of a dead man who wishes to practise rites of regeneration enters into a ritual identification with Shu, one of the gods of Becoming/creation—who was also breathing itself, luminosity, *and the emptiness of the void* (Willems, 1996: 197–209). The son, in identification with Shu, directs a spell of regeneration to the amulet hung about his dead father's neck, and he invokes the spirit of his father as Atum, who is the sun-god father of Shu.

Respiration is the epitome of cosmos; it reveals, more than any other sensory function does, how cosmos is everything and nothing within the drawing in and expulsion of a breath. Shu, as god of breathing, is the god of nothing (one of the meanings of the concept "shu"). But his state of embodiment indicates intuitions of a theological kind concerning fusion: he and his father Atum are consubstantial (the Coffin texts must be the first record of this doctrine); and both he and his father claim to be self-created.[5]

Becoming in this conception is without subject or object,[6] originating as a potential without constraint (transference as *prayer*). So also the organs of the senses, as derived from metaphysical conceptions of *hearing, seeing, touching,* and so forth, are without subject and object. Father and son—basically a dyad of imaginary twins—describe an act of breathing, which hangs in the air as it were, as it forms into a spectral presence.

Among the ancient Greeks, types of thinking of an *existence itself* kind are projected into phantasies concerning the powers of divine metamorphosis, in which gods escape from the regulations of the body by turning to volatile states of transformation. Some of the ancient Greeks appear to have intuited the conflict that arises when the sequentiality of the Euclidean conception of space, as the ground for an inexorable logic or "proof", is opposed to the vagaries of metaphysical space and claimed to be the one means to truth.[7]

Notes

1. That the culture of the bone (Adam's rib) should transform into the culture of the relic (the matrix of silence, personified by the body of Eve) raises a structuralist question concerning the disappearance of either bones or *axis mundi* in myth and rite (viz. the disappearance of the bones of the sacrificed camel among the desert people).

2. "There is one story and one story only / That will prove worth your telling, / Whether as learned hard or gifted child" (Robert Graves, "To Juan at the Winter Solstice", 1948: 220).

3. In other words, within this interpretation Pythagoras and the black smith at his forge are aspects of the same representation of the divine king.

4. Within the membrane, father and son are barely differentiated constituents.

5. Spell 75 in the Coffin texts (Faulkner, 1973), from which I take this myth, rings the peals on the concept of Becoming, which is also in part the concept of self-creation.

6. The essence of a transference without subject or object is *prayer*. The sacrifice and prayer are aspects of each other.

7. A first-born son has to smash open his father's skull during the rites of a Hindu cremation. The sun, rising in a blaze of light, creates an emblem for time that the Platonic imagination may perceive to be an icon for the indeterminate. In myth the incandescence of skull and of sun might be read as indicators of renewal.

15

*Fusion, separation,
& the contact barrier*

In many African traditions of kingship, the ritual murder
of one king and the initiation of another king are stages in
the same ceremony: the emerging of two bodies out of a
state of fusion signals the death of one of the bodies in order
that time might be renewed. The initiate king, in reviving the
royal calendar, eats the heart of the dead king. And he is
married, if only for one night, to one of the wives of the dead
king.

An ancient Greek ritual, in which a priest wears a Janus-
headed mask made up of a face of the old king, facing backward,
and the face of the young king, facing forward, offers a similar
construction, by binding the two kings in a ceremony of death-
in-life and life-in-death.

A red-figured bell-*kratér* from Ruvo shows Hermes attacking
Argos. This ritual scene represents not only the killing of the
old king, but also apparently part of the ritual of Sacred
Marriage. The king wears a double-headed mask, which
presents an old bearded face to the attacker and a young face
to the goddess, to whom he is making advances. The young
face is perhaps a survival of the beardless Zeus Velcanos;

moreover, *the body of the king is covered with eyes*, and in this respect is similar to certain representations of the Cretan Minotaur-king. He wears a leopard skin, associated in Egypt and elsewhere only with royal and divine persons. The goddess is horned, symbolizing her relationship with the sacred cow, which points to a connection with Egypt. Argos himself shows certain affinities with the king-gods of Asia Minor, by wearing the double head and brandishing the club of Hercules. It is evident that the sacrificer came to be known as Hermes. In later history we shall find that Hermes' head was combined with that of Hercules or of Dionysus as a double head on coins, and consequently associated with a royal dynasty. Pausanias says that Hermes *is a servant of Zeus, and leads down the spirits of the departed to Hades.* [Deedes, 1935: 215–216]

The murdered twin is similar to the Greek god Dionysus, in the sense that he is restricted to travelling between the terrestrial and the subterrestrial realm of the dead; he is not allowed access to the heavens. But his twin has eye and star motifs on his garments; he is a creature of the sky; and the pattern of eyes–stars on his cloak engages with the fused figure as though it marked the entry of some third element into the dyad. A brilliant night sky, as an indeterminate space (indeterminacy being represented by the two-dimensionality of the plane surface), separates the figures of sacrificer and sacrificed. The star–eyes on the cloak of the initiate king is reminiscent of A. B. Cook's (1904) descriptions of Zeus as a triple-eyed god, two of whose eyes evoke the harmony of sun and moon, while a third and cyclopean eye, like Milton's concept of *blind mouth*, is a metaphysical space in between, such as an infant might imagine to occur as it travels through the indeterminate space between the feeding breasts.

In terms of one interpretation of the contact barrier, *gap* indicates death and descent into the underworld, the threshold as a site of fragmentation, while *link* indicates a release into the night skies. In some circumstances, gaps gives rise to links, thresholds, and to means of communication through such labyrinthine communicators as the stars of the night sky, or the light in a mother's gaze. One twin potentially is either a father, or a son, in a state of bringing to life the other twin, who is a son or a father. Within this interpretation of the contact barrier, the presence of a mother in the dyad is barely perceptible.

The object of sacrifice, the king who must die, in being everything and nothing, centre and void, is comparable to a placental membrane, on whose surface appear signs. Tattoo markings would seem to emerge from *within the skin*. The ancient Egyptian dwarf-god Bes, as liminal in nature as the Janus-headed figure, has a body marked with *wadjet* eye signs. The writing, which the Gourmantché expect to see on the skin of the victim during the act of dismemberment, appears as spontaneously as the signs that arise through the earth's surface during the rites of geomantic divination. The future, as it enters into the present, has the form of a generative void.

In traditional cosmology, signs emerge by way of *a sacred body that is everything or nothing*, a concept that gives rise to the icon as an object of wonder. The group that practises the sacrifice has to displace the victim from centre to periphery. In this way, the sacred king at the centre is also identified with formless and malformed figures on the periphery, spectres from the netherworld, who exist in the wilderness outside the village, or the empire.

In sign-thinking, duration is contingent in its relation to the categories of time. It arises out of a void which is inseparable from conceptions of the future. In any culture in which "duration" is in the process of formation, all action is a form of promise which awaits realisation, an idea of the future as "a legacy without testament" (Char, 1944: 102). Diviners among the Dogon think of paw-mark patternings left on the ground by the jackal (who is associated with incest, as well as liminality) as though the jackal were the future speaking to the present with a mouth that devours the inhabitants of the present (Griaule, 1937; Paulme, 1937). The future stakes out the "distances" of the present by seeming to emerge through a sacred terrain conceived of as a membrane.

16

Centre & void as reciprocals

An idea of breakdown, as an inseparable function of creativity, is fundamental to the means by which traditional cosmology articulates itself. Iconism and myth require discontinuity in order to create forms of continuity—as though discovering plenitude in negation. The metaphysical threshold that signs cross as they form is more than zero as sign: it has to be associated with the cataclysmic power of zero as symbol—contact barrier as related to the becoming of "O", and not contact barrier as a means of linkage that accommodates the threats of the gap. In the cosmology implied by Spinoza's *existence itself*, the metaphysical threshold, or contact barrier—in this case, as constituted of Plato's metaphysical space—lies between *existence itself* and the inexplicable manifestations of the "forms of life". In the more neutralised conception of the contact barrier, gap gives rise to linkage, threshold to labyrinth, and acts of sacrifice to an unaccountable series of markings or tattooings on the skin, which can come close to being zero as symbol. A variant on this kind of sign making, which occurs on a plane surface, is called by Lévi-Strauss (1944) *dédoublement*—or, in English translation, *split representation*.

71

> Split representation in Northwest Coast art has been de-
> scribed by Franz Boas as follows: "The animal is imagined
> cut in two from head to tail . . . there is a deep depression
> between the eyes, extending down the nose. This shows that
> the head itself must not have been considered a front view,
> but as consisting of two profiles which adjoin at mouth and
> nose, while they are not in contact with each other on a level
> with the eyes and forehead . . . either the animals are repre-
> sented as split in two so that the profiles are joined in the
> middle, or a front view of the head is shown with two adjoin-
> ing profiles of the body." [Lévi-Strauss, 1944: 248]

Many cultures provide examples of objects that, in having been
split into plane surfaces, then have the plane surfaces relate to
each other like reflections in a mirror. The "hinging" of the two
reflections creates a triadic object out of the dyad reflection. The
"hinging" indicates the presence of the contact barrier in its
non-catastrophic aspect. But if the mirror should transform into
the oceanic depths of the imaginative, as described by Shakespeare in *The Tempest*, then the effect of the reflections on each
other can be catastrophic. By assuming a different cosmological
domain from the one who looks into it, the mirror, in becoming
the oceans' depth, destroys the gaze of the other. Lévi-Strauss
refers to a myth in which a sacred gaze, with the authority of
the oceanic and the properties of the imagination, inadvertently
annihilates a human gaze.

> Six anthropomorphic supernatural beings . . . emerged from
> the ocean to mingle with human beings. One of them had his
> eyes covered and dared not look at the Indians, though he
> showed the greatest anxiety to do so. At last he could no
> longer restrain his curiosity, and on one occasion he partially
> lifted his veil, and his eye fell on the form of a human being,
> who instantly fell dead "as if struck by one of the thunderers."
> Though the intentions of this dread being were friendly to
> men, yet the glance of his eye was too strong, and it inflicted
> certain death. His fellows therefore caused him to return
> to the bosom of the great water. The five others remained
> among the Indians, and "became a blessing to them." From
> them originate the five great clans or totems: catfish, crane,
> loon, bear, and marten. [Lévi-Strauss, 1962b: 19]

In "an experiment used in schools to demonstrate the propagation of light in straight lines", writes Lévi-Strauss (1958: 184), a pin-hole, as disjunctive transformer, inverts light-rays that pass through it and by this means increases their intensity. The weakening state of the light-rays that enter the pin-hole corresponds in intensity to their revitalised state as they leave it. The contrasted intensities of light-rays are a counterpart in optics to the mythic conflict in gaze of the sea-god and the human gaze, or to the belief in traditional cosmology that a cosmos moving into negation might enter into conflict with a cosmos moving into plenitude. The observer of the movement of light-rays through a pin-hole might be inclined to divide what is in fact one set of light-rays into two sets of light-rays.

> An image can be seen in full detail when observed through any adequately large aperture. But as the aperture is narrowed, the image becomes blurred and difficult to see. When, however, the aperture is further reduced to a pinpoint, that is to say, when communication is about to vanish, the image is inverted and becomes clear again. This experiment is used in schools to demonstrate the propagation of light in straight lines—in other words, to prove that rays of light are not transmitted at random but within the limits of a structured field. [Lévi-Strauss, 1958: 184]

In 1956, Lévi-Strauss described a similar configuration in terms of village structures, in which the relation of moieties, although seemingly binary in structure, had a triadic significance. He thought that breakdown in the relationship between the moieties could be delayed, possibly for ever, by the significance that each moiety granted to the zero function of the boundary between them. He did not contend that the boundary, as a variable without content, might have the absolute potency of "O"—that it might be a sign transformed into a symbol. He thought that it might be no more than an expediency; and in this sense, he did not do justice to the range of his idea, which makes sense as a way of conceptualising the idea of the *yantra*, a type of inscape that intensifies the contemplative abilities of those who look into it. The idea that Lévi-Strauss indicates can be read in such a way that zero, rather than representing nothing, can represent the power of a disjunctive transformer, a contact-barrier threshold that is the source for *an image in form* so inducing of unknowing that it might be assumed to be have a universal significance.[1]

In traditional cosmology, the making of any object arises from the act of its disintegration. Without creation, there is no sacrifice; without sacrifice, there is no act of creation. And this binding together of extreme possibilities is implicit in any movement. All change or transformation—in utmost neurosis—intimates annihilation.

> The prince of Makari was a near recluse. Thinking himself to be a cosmic pivot, he did not dare leave his house, in case he wrenched out of place the axis of the cosmos. [Lebeuf, 1973: 448]

All change or transformation intimates disintegration. Lévi-Strauss discovered images of *dédoublement* in cultures as distant from each other as middle America and ancient China; and he saw its likeness in the craft of tattooing. The drawing of a single and continuous line, which takes on the mirror patterning of a labyrinth, can occur, as an antidote to interruption and surcease, in cultures as remote from each other as that of Vanuatu in the Pacific and Tamilnadu in south India (see chapter 23). The labyrinth as link–gap in this context indicates a dangerous crossing between two realms, often by water (prebirth into birth, death into afterlife). In the interpretation of traditional cosmology, the gap is a negation of plenitude, while the link, of indeterminate length, is plenitude as the fulfilment of creation—intimating the unpredictable or labyrinthine operations of grace.

Note

1. J. S. Bach thought of himself as a follower of Pythagoras; and the conviction that proportionality is *one universal idea* in all art might occur to anyone who is open to the range in dimensionality with which Bach works out musical form. This is to be contained within the movement of the constellations in the night sky.

17

The Word as ear–mouth

A victim is sacrificed—a man, or by substitution, an animal.
A sacred text is read out in a loud voice, and those who have
participated in the sacrifice add their voices to it. Or this rite
is carried out before a plate of precious metal on which there
lies one of the victim's severed ears. It is the ear to whom the
sacred text is uttered. It is clear that at this moment the ear
has become the ear of the god. The victim has given the
formless god a personality by way of an ear. [Mus, 1933: 375][1]

In this rite, the severance of an ear initiates the distinction
between god and man, and between the heavens and the
earth.[2] But the rite also draws attention to some fundamental state of non-differentiation, out of which the possibilities of
differentiation might arise. The ear of the sacrifice in this case
is an ear–mouth in which hearing and utterance are inseparable. The membrane of this kind of ear, like the membrane of a
drum, allows exit, as well as entry, to timbre. To communicate
with the gods requires the drum of the ear–mouth, which is a
version of Bion's "optic pit". Fundamental to the emergence of
function—specifically, of the personality as functioning within
the Cartesian spectrum of self and other, mind and body, sub-

75

ject and object—is the ear–mouth as optic pit. A non-differen-tiated state of hearing and uttering is relevant to the means by which subject and object separate. If interpreted as a meta-physical phenomenon or poetic symbol, the ear–mouth as optic pit is the means that underwrites the existence of the capacity to perceive. Without the presence of "O" as poetic symbol, this means remains inoperative.

In certain rituals, the transformation of the sacrifice into creation originates symbolically within the human ear as micro-cosm. An ear, in acquiring sacral qualities through severance from a body, can originate the quarters.

> Whenever the cosmos is created, the body is destroyed and—conversely—whenever the body is created, the cosmos is de-stroyed. . . . As one exhales, breath leaves the body through the nose and enters the wind, leaving the wind and rejoining the body upon inhalation. The simple act of breathing thus alternately constructs the macrocosm (while deconstructing the microcosm), then constructs the microcosm (while deconstructing the macrocosm). Similarly, as sound travels into the distance and ceases to be heard, the cardinal direc-tions (the utmost statement of spatial distance) come into being as the sound enters them, while the ears fall apart, being no longer in use. But when sound travels from the distance and is heard by the ears, distance ceases to be, and the ears are reconstituted through the act of hearing. [Lin-coln, 1986: 33–35]

Sacred formulas accompany the act of dismemberment:

> Lay its feet down to the north. Cause its eye to go to the sun; send forth its breath to the wind; its life-force to the atmos-phere; its ear to the cardinal points; its flesh to the earth. Thus (the dismemberer) places this (animal) in these worlds. . . .
>
> The moon was born of his mind; of his eye, the sun was born. From his mouth, Indra and fire; from his breath, wind was born. From his navel there was the atmosphere; from his head, heaven was rolled together; from his feet, the earth; from his ear, the cardinal directions. Thus they cause the world to be created. [Lincoln, 1986: 58, quoting from the *Rg Veda*]

The orients, as four quarters, invite the imaginative conjecture that the victim of the sacrifice, before differentiation, has a Janus-head, with four ears and four eyes. By way of the act of severance, the victim's four ears transfigure into the four ear–orients. Adam's rib, as an object of the sacrifice, is metamorphic in a similar way, although it transfigures into the presence of Eve, rather than into the presence of the orients. The severed ear–mouth, or rib, as *axis mundi*, represents the domains of the various orients.

But the ear, as well as being an agent for the poetic symbol, functions in a dual way, in the sense that it acts as a means of proprioceptive equilibration, as well as a means for monitoring the location of sound in space. Otto Isakower (1939) proposed that the duality of the auditory system, *by the very fact of its duality*, was essential to the evolution of Freud's theory of the superego.

> In the first of Freud's two sketches, made in 1923, in *The Ego and the Id* . . . [1923b], the ego has on one side "an auditory lobe" ["Hörkappe", literally, "cap of hearing"] "worn crooked". In the repetition of this sketch, which appeared in 1933 in his *New Introductory Lectures* . . . [1933a] and which in other respects is practically unaltered, this "auditory lobe" is no longer to be seen. The corresponding position is now occupied by the super-ego. [Isakower, 1939: 348]

Within the membrane of an eardrum, or cosmologically within the membrane of actual drums and tambourines as microcosms or sonar cosmic systems, lies the strange authority that Freud categorised as that of the superego. Agents for the achievement of ethical, as well as physical, equilibrium would appear to come into being as personifications of a certain limited spatial intuition, which excludes intuitions of metaphysical space and which is inclined to re-direct thought from thinking by way of signs to thinking by way of the writing conception.

The dwarf as superego.   Dwarfs can represent the authority of the superego by their physical likeness to a severed ear. The ancient Egyptian creationist god, Ptah, is an ear dwarf as well as being the god worshipped by craftsmen. Being the *ear that speaks* is comparable to creating the Word in thought and then transforming the thought into matter. The Memphis creationist myth, as recorded on the Shabaka stone in the British Museum, specifically describes the creationist abilities of Ptah as *acts of hearing*.

The ear, like the eye, is able to register the Cartesian "distinct", as well as the Cartesian "clear", in that it provides the body with two types of bearing (equilibrium and the location of sensation). In severance, it is like the Cartesian severed limb, in which sensation, although "clear", is indistinct and therefore liable to be understood either as hallucination or as angelic vision. An ear and eye that register the "clear" and not the "distinct" will alternate sense information in the Pythagorean manner, by which a silent celestial *visuality* can render imaginatively *audible* an imperceptible music of the stars, or the noise of a terrestrial smithy can render imaginatively visible an intuition of universal form. Relevant to the forming of this *yantra*, or instrument for aesthetic introspection, is the alternating structure by which the five points situated at the zenith and at the orients transform into functions "at the centre".

The auricular membrane conducts different sites into the human body: one such site is the nether world of the unappeased dead; another such site is the heavenly sphere of the Platonic forms. The movement of constellations in the night sky intimates the nature of the heavenly forms as the source from which originates beauty in the world. Patterns unfold within the whorl of an ear. The Janus-head notion that there might be at some stage four ears and therefore four voices (four grandparents or four grandchildren) informs the legend in which a king, who has lapsed into disgrace, is upheld by the orients represented by his four grandsons (Dumézil, 1971: 30 et seq.).

In creationism, the ear of the victim of the sacrifice originates the equilibrium of the quarters. Ontologically the skin on a shaman's drum is no different from the membrane of a sacral ear, which in its listening can also speak. When the shaman beats his drum, he is able, by the sound of the drum-beat, to draw into the drum's skin the ghosts of the newly dead who dangerously roam the world of the living when unconfined (Meuli, 1935: 124). This is one example of the superego as an ancestral presence that must be confined if it is not to be destructive.[3] In phantasy, the dead are most dangerous as ghosts when they escape from the aural site of the Freudian superego.

The aural membrane is a two-dimensional representation of a place in which the ancestors—who possibly have been mutilated in dying—must be kept, if the living are to live in peace. A failure to include all the ancestors within the aural membrane may be one of the "bad properties of the ear" associated with dwarfs other than Ptah (see chapter 19). In Dogon mythology the skull, rather than the ear, of the dismembered water-spirit Nommo activates a transformation, which results in the appearance of the first cosmogram for creation itself, which is an actual drum.

Notes

1. "The grotesque body . . . is a body in the act of becoming. It is never finished, never completed. . . . The artistic logic of the grotesque image ignores the closed, smooth, impenetrable surface of the body and retains only its excrescencies (sprouts, buds) and orifices, only that which lends beyond the body's limited space or into the body's depths. The primacy and potency of the grotesque lie in its association with ideas of displeasure, *disequilibrium* and change" (Bakhtin, 1968, in Blier, 1995: 2; emphasis added).

2. Hesiod's account of how Kronos castrates his heavenly father Ouranos and, by separating the heavens from the earth, disrupts Ouranos' unceasing congress with Gaia as mother-earth is a relevant model for this act of division.

3. Poisoning by ear is a motif in Shakespeare's *Hamlet*. It is represented by a "dumb" show, in which one brother poisons another. It is also represented by a dead father who wreaks havoc and poisons Hamlet's ear because he has not been confined to a nether-world—in microcosm, the membrane of an eardrum, or the membrane of any drum of death. Arguably, music is a form of silence that confines dangerous presences within the emissions of tempered sounds. It liberates danger only then to encage it within the forms of pulse.

18

"A lack of precision in mediaeval descriptions, not only of architectural patterns, but of all geometric forms"

Science for certain of the ancient Greeks was correct categorisation; and this entailed correct localisation: there was no conscious desire for maps of the Holy Spirit, *in which distance is a variable*. In this way, Greek cosmology differs from many other traditional cosmologies. In Platonism, truth is distinct as well as clear. The great discovery of metaphysical space implies some recognition of an *existence itself*, which might be "indistinct" because it is without location and without representation, but Plato appears to draw back from exploring the implications of his great discovery. If he had explored the idea of metaphysical space, he might have arrived at definitions of space that would have opposed the movement in his culture towards the formalisation of the type of space on which Euclid was to depend.[1] Plato anticipates Euclidean space and in this anticipation loses sight of metaphysical space as the meaningfully random. The shapes that the demiurge in the *Timaeus* draws out of the *anima mundi* by dissection are definable and knowable archetypes without which, in Platonic hypothesis, there could be no existence. The basic building blocks of the cosmos exist in some prior fashion to the existence of the cosmos; and Plato's sacred geometry does not differ from Euclid's geometry in postulating such priorities. Chance, or non-differentiation, as arising from the threshold of the aniconic, play no creative part in this activity. Definable counters of thought are the *fons et origo* of existence. It is as though Plato intimated the concept of the Holy Spirit in his definition of metaphysical space and then sought to take flight from this intuition.[2]

But in other cultures, the idea of the Holy Spirit provides a context for certain non-Platonic hypotheses of a Platonic kind: for instance, that the foetus might be able to bear witness to the presence of light before its eyes have formed, or that its mother first "sees" it by way of an act of hearing—as in the mystery of the Annunciation. Conceivably, the foetus is able to "hear" the light before it has acquired an organ for hearing. (And yet this idea, so fundamental to the Pythagorean impulse, exists in some buried fashion in the Platonic imagination.)

When asked to draw a square, certain people in the Middle Ages drew a circle; or, when asked to draw a circle, they drew a square (Krautheimer, 1942: 1–33). There is a "peculiar lack of precision in mediaeval descriptions not only of architectural patterns but of all geometric forms" (ibid.: 7). Conceivably, these people had lost the armature on which the existence of their bodies depended; and they were haunted by the idea of a lost centre as an object of wonder—an absence that invoked a painful yearning. They conceived of the lost armature as a magical space in which the dead are reborn, and they saw the lost centre in unexpected places. Some of them insisted that a baptistery, with no physical likeness to the Holy Sepulchre in Jerusalem, was a "copy" of the Holy Sepulchre in Jerusalem. Similarly, the architecture of the Holy Sepulchre, as an image of proportion, was so informed by the passion of loss that some people saw it in improbable places. In a similar identification with the idea of death and rebirth, Shakespeare's Ferdinand was transfigured by an idea of his seemingly drowned father.[3]

Mind's eclipse in the act of sacrifice signifies the merging of forms as they disappear: objects of Becoming retreat into some indefinable condition of Being. A traveller, dying of thirst in some desert of the mind, has an oscillating perception of a mirage, which yet might be an oasis. The idea of a "centre" that is everything or nothing—as a way of describing the formation of a concept, or as a way of describing the formation of a god, which personifies such a concept, or as a way of describing the formation of a god's habitation as an aspect of the god's body—presumes the idea of a map in which distance is a variable.

A conviction wells up in the group mind concerning the transfiguration of a "sacral" body out of nothingness—the body appears as a corporeity of supernatural intensity. As actuality, its resurrection is a form of magic; in thought, it is a poetic symbol that typifies the Coleridgean imagination.[4] In Freudian terms, secondary process fails: the ego, unable to register differences in the object accurately, finds itself tantalised by an extraordinary belief in the value of "copying"—and of copying something that the "copy" in no way resembles, as though insisting that something that is without resemblance is a copy of the copy. "Copying" of this kind underlies the formation of that type of transference, which Freud interpreted as facsimile. And yet it appears to be a function of inspiration—or of what Freud at one time thought of as hysteria.

Space suited to represent the disjunctive element in ontological transformation is a metaphysical space. Only sacred signs can pass through this fiery furnace. In the *Timaeus*, sacred geometry is separated from the site of sacral terror, although it is structured as though it were an act of sacrifice. Sacral terror, if acknowledged, challenges the postulates of reason.

Manners of transformation in which the concept of duration plays no part, which occur before the formation of shapes, and which remain on the verge of representation, would seem to tremble and waver in the sea's depths, where the body of a non-existent king is transfigured. There are no fixities and definites in this space, and its logic does not submit to the authority of geometric forms. And yet in terms of the transformation of Being into Becoming, the sign system of such a geometry must pass through a stage in formation in which it shows itself to be a variable in a state of metamorphosis. In such an "indistinct" condition, a square and a circle might be taken to be one or the other. Lévi-Strauss, in writing about *mana*, or zero function, suggests that

> we are not dealing with a universal and permanent form of thought, which, far from characterising certain civilisations, or archaic or semi-archaic so-called "stages" in the evolution of the human mind, [is] a certain way which the mind situates itself in the presence of things, and which must therefore make an appearance whenever that mental situation is given. [Lévi-Strauss, 1950: 53]

Notes

1. And which Bion was to point to as the paradigm of how erroneous thinking operates in psychoanalysis.

2. However, the ancient Greeks were drawn to images of metamorphosis and fluidity in the divine; and although they idealised a certain norm concerning types of human beauty, they did have also, through their conception of divine volatility, some intimation of the sacred body as everything and nothing.

3. Shakespeare's transfiguring of the non-existent drowned king describes the *significance* of such initiatory rites as baptism.

4. The radical transformations of Coleridge's Imagination are founded in concrete-equation thinking. "The primary IMAGINATION I hold to be the living Power and Prime Agent of all human Perception, and as a repetition in the finite mind of the eternal act of creation in the infinite I AM."

19

The body of the king as the calendar of his people

One of the architectural representations of the contact barrier is the bridge: this is the contact barrier as enabler. Another such representation of the contact barrier is the altar: this is contact barrier as the architecture of catastrophic change. Both are ways of relating links and gaps. The bridge, like a metaphor, links one knowable place to another knowable place. The altar, like the icon, links the site of the sacrifice to some unknowable domain "on the other side". It is as though a mirror were no longer to reflect an image in glass but to reveal some oceanic state of otherness, which the terrestrial finds unimaginable. A counterpart for the bridge is the event, which consists of a beginning, a middle, and an end. A counterpart for the altar is the rite of passage, which consists of a death, an indeterminate transition, and a "rebirth". The contact barrier, which functions as an enabling link, and the contact barrier as the source of catastrophic change, are aspects of the same means of symbolisation.

The significance of the altar as rite of passage informs the disjunctive location of the divine king—wherever the location might be, within the palace, or at every point throughout the

kingdom. And it informs the disjunctive nature of the royal
body, which is constituted of two or more bodies existing within
the same time span, therefore making the divine king a guard-
ian of twinship. One body is heavenly and the other is terrestrial; one is everything, and the other is nothing; one is the
centre, and the other is the periphery. Ritual puts the divine
king under pressure to be both himself and yet many others.

Through the instrumentality of the altar, the void as symbol
assumes the forms that constitute the signs of duration; and by
way of the altar, the divine king's body is able to become the
calendar of his people. But if the king's sovereignty is weak, if he
fails to be initiated out of the body of a dead king, he may remain
isolated from the gap–link's power to engender time schemes.
Arguably, this was the case with Seti I, whose right to the throne
of ancient Egypt was open to dispute, and whose cenotaph at
Abydos (Frankfort, 1933) reveals a split representation in relation to time. In parallel to the depiction of Re's diurnal progression through death and rebirth by way of the body of his mother,
the sky-goddess Nut, the cenotaph also gives a practical account
of how a gnomon–clock works. The king's body exists in corre-
spondence with, and yet in separation from, the gnomon–clock.
His body has not acquired the cosmic instrumentality of being
time's marker within the context of the kingdom.

The gnomon is inoperative during the hours of darkness and
during some of the hours of light; and to this extent, it is like the
body of the sun-king, as it awaits rebirth in the tomb–womb of
a sky-goddess. It is like a favoured toy, laid by the body of a dead
child-king.

Types of feigning, often associated with acting and folklore,
may play some part in the initiation of temporality. Under strict
conditions, a scapegoat can take the place of the projected victim. Chronos, wishing to eat his son Zeus, does not realise
that he is about to ingest a swaddled stone. Possibly the camel,
which the desert people slaughtered and ate during the time
of first light (chapter 13), was a surrogate for the principal and
imperceptible dwarf-god of Becoming, the scarab beetle Khepri.[1]
The hands on a huge and imaginary clock, in pointing at the
terrestrial camel, also indicate, in a covert fashion, the imperceptible and *celestial* figure of the scarab beetle as solar regenera-

tor. The day re-begins in a blaze of glory because the infant god
of Becoming has been put to the sacrifice.

> Egyptian religion was deeply concerned with maintaining
> the order of the created world, always threatened by the
> primeval chaos, outside and within creation, full of mon-
> strous hybrid beings. Dwarfs, although malformed, do not
> seem to have been assimilated to these disturbing and
> threatening creatures. Their liminality was made symboli-
> cally acceptable by association with positive religious con-
> cepts. From the New Kingdom on, and probably earlier, they
> emerge as popular deities, best known in their forms of Bes
> and Ptah-Pataikoi. . . . [Dasen, 1993: 46]

Signs must be fragmented in order to be re-formed. Physical
deformity, like the dismemberment of the king's body, indicates
the liminal element in contact-barrier theory. In travesty of the
link, the king is obliged to enter into the premature linkage of
incestuous relationships; in travesty of the gap, his body must
be eviscerated on death. The forming of the schemas of duration
exacts a price that the body of the divine king has to bear.

The gap–link conjunction operates by circular, rather than
by linear, means. The murder of a predecessor sacralises the
king—but he, in turn, must renew sacrality by his own submission to the sacrifice. The circularity of the conjoined gap–link
revitalises the significance of the sacrificial act. "In most magical texts, dwarfs appear as manifestations of the sun-god Re . . .
they are described as rising up into the sky and going down to
the underworld" (Dasen, 1993: 46). In disappearing behind the
horizon and into concealment, the dwarf–infant assumes the
conditions of the buried dead. "The small scarab [is great]
through its secret image, the small dwarf is great because of his
name" (ibid.: 50). And yet their eyes can take the form of the sun
and the moon. "A New Kingdom flask depicts the god dwarf Bes.
He holds an eye in either hand" (ibid.).

In the wilderness, far from the site in which culture fabri-
cates mirror images of its own nature, the dwarf Bes presides
over acts of parturition and oceanic makings of music. "The
protective role of Bes during and after delivery is relevant to his
strong relationship with music" (ibid.: 78). By way of his dance,

time itself forms into a solar progression and discloses how music and time are aspects of each other. The *wadjet* eyes on Bes' cloak are comparable to the garment covered in eyes on the Janus-headed god (Deedes, 1935) (see chapter 15).[2]

Contact-barrier thinking can intimate, without articulating, the idea of an inspiration by which a culture makes the objects that reflect its own image. Ptah, as Ptah-Pataikoi, another dwarf, is a god of inspiration, as well as of craft, a precursor of the Greek blacksmith-god dwarf, Hephaestus.

> The image of Hephaestus is most like to the Phoenicians' [*Ptah-*] *Pataikoi*, which the Phoenicians carry on the prows of their triremes. I will describe it for him who has not seen these figures: *it is in the likeness of a pygmy.* [Herodotus 3.37, in Dasen, 1993: 84][3]

Ptah represents

> . . . the creative function of thought, utterance and informa-tion. . . .
> The opening words of John's Gospel, devoid of their Christian implications, could easily have been appreciated by the Egyptian author(s) of the "Memphite Theology" as a summary of their own view of the creation. *In the beginning was the Word.* . . . [Allen, 1988: 46]

> The young scribe learnt hieratic at school, and this is what the Egyptians understood to be writing. The study of hieroglyphs was restricted to craftsmen who specialised in the decoration of monuments and whose god, Ptah, created the world by means that were intellectual as well as iconic and verbal. In creating the form of things, Ptah invented their design, which is their image and their name, and which is the phonetic of the image, and functions as a sign. The thoughts of the heart are expressed verbally by language and visibly by the sign-image. [Assmann, 2000: 116]

Hieroglyphs, as *divine speech*, as visual images, resemble the *wadjet* eyes, which appear on Bes' body. They are not writing, although they may operate by way of sequence. They are wrought, as though in the smithy. In intention, if not in fact, they enact the silent eloquence of the music of the spheres.

The severed body of the victim of the sacrifice initiates music and art, as well as time: a rite of passage that is inseparable from any act of iconic making. Pythagoras discovers a music in dissonance, by way of a celestial domain, which offers a rite of passage through death, and which purges dissonance, so that a pattern might be realised. The Word is identified with the sacred dwarf-gods of Khepri, Ptah, and Bes, who are intermediaries between existence itself and the idea of sequence. The cosmic instrumentality of the extracted rib in the legend of Adam's sacrifice is evocative of the power of the dwarf-gods. The doctrine that words equal (wrought) things, or that (wrought) things equal words, is here bound up with the doctrines of the sacrifice, in which the ear that hears can be also the ear that speaks (see chapter 17).

The dwarf's dance.   Spell 517 in the Pyramid texts (Faulkner, 1969: 191) is a rite of rebirth. The speaker of the sacred words appears to be a priest, possibly the king himself, who describes an act of ascension, which he may also enact in sacred drama. The king in death swims to an isle[4] within the thighs of his mother Nut. As a *dng*, which is possibly a dwarf, he delights a great god (whose name remains undisclosed) by performing a dance of the gods before the god's throne. In streets and houses of an unknown location, this act is celebrated.

In dying, Khepri initiates time by releasing the sun-god, who crosses the horizon and brings into being time in the form of a play of shadows the movement of which registers time for the earth dwellers.[5] In an analogue, a dwarf who dances before the king ritually unites the king both with sacred temporality and with music.

During the predynastic period at least one king (the king known as Den) danced before the throne of a great god.[6] Conceivably a priest, Khepri, in the act of solar regeneration, represents both the dwarf who dances and the great god seated on his throne, the sacrificed and the sacrificer. The priest is also Re as the sun-god, enshrined between two mountain peaks, about to make his glorious diurnal ascent. The priest marks the separation between the god as imaginary twin (Khepri) and the god as newborn (Re). The celebration in the houses and streets of the royal city below marks the beginnings of day.

The rite does not describe the notion that in birth one aspect of the newborn, the imaginary twin, must be sacrificed. And yet Maspero (1893) has indicated that Erman had earlier identified the *dng* not with the regenerative, but with the dead, and that he had identified the *ahket*, as the environment of the *dng*, with the kingdom of the dead. This is to assume some compatibility between the western horizon over which the sun disappears (the place of death) and the eastern horizon over which the sun rises (the place of birth). In cosmological significance, the two horizons are one horizon, the place of death being the place of rebirth.[7]

In Saussure's terms, *dng* and *ahket* are variable signs performing a zero function, which enables a sign system to operate. The *dng* personifies the *ahket*. Maspero (1893) has pointed out that the association of *dng* and *ahket* occurs in another context, which is historical rather than mythological: in a letter in which a scribe, writing on behalf of the child-king Pepy II, encourages the king's emissary, Harkhuf, to bring back a *dng* from the land of the blessed. Harkhuf thought this letter valuable enough, in regard to his justification in the afterlife, to have it inscribed on the walls inside his tomb.

> Come north to the residence at once! Hurry and bring with you this pygmy whom you brought from the land of the horizon-dwellers live, hale, and healthy, for the dances of the god, to gladden the heart, to delight the heart of King Neferkare who lives forever. When he goes down with you into the ship, get worthy men to be around him on deck, lest he fall into the water! When he lies down at night, get worthy men to lie around him in his tent. Inspect him ten times at night! My majesty desires to see this *dng* more than the gifts of Sinai and of Punt. [in Lichtheim, 1975: 27]

Presumably, the child-king wants to appropriate the *dng* as a playmate who is as small as he is; but conceivably, on a liturgical level, the king requires the *dng* as a means of incorporating Khepri within himself, and therefore of incorporating time, so that he might be the calendar of his people. The king's relationship to Being is a prerogative of his kingship; but he must also acquire, through the *dng* as Khepri, a power glimpsed in acts of solar regeneration and in the art of dancing, *which is time as a function of inspiration,* or, in Plato's terms, time as an icon of eternity (which Seti I is thought to have failed to acquire: hence the separation of the gnomon–clock from any iconism associated with his body).

Appropriating the powers of the *dng*, and of the god-dance, enhances the powers of sovereignty; and this appropriation derives from a culture that idealises the craftsman as a maker of icons. Time, described in terms of the art of dancing, is a wrought and aesthetic object: it is the sacred calendar, which the body of the king must incorporate if he is to create a music sweet to the ears of the people of his kingdom.

Khepri "dies" in order that daily the sun-god Re might be reborn. Similarly, in the ancient Greek myth of Pollux and Castor, Pollux saves his twin Castor from extirpation by giving him a lease on his own immortality: one twin must half-die in order that the other twin might half-live. In granting Castor some measure of his immortality, Pollux is able to assume the pulse of time. (Through the "biting" of the beaver Castor, Pollux begins to breathe.) The twins represent not so much a *gap* between Being and Becoming as a dioscuric mirroring across an abyss. When zero as sign loses its individuality (in repairing the deteriorated system), it "dies" in order to undergo restoration, and in this way zero as sign is transfigured into zero as symbol.[8]

The operations of the Word oppose the presumptions that the well-regulated body imposes on thought. Descartes comes closest to the doctrine of the Word, and to the dismemberment of the sacrifice, when he considers the meaning of referred pain in a body from which a leg has been severed. It is when body rebels against ideas of perfection in function that it begins to disclose its affinity to the wayward nature of the symbol.

As a divinity who presides over first light, Khepri is related to visuality. But by way of Ptah, he is related to the importance that the Memphis creation myth ascribes to sound.[9] Khepri is the ear, as well as the eye, of the sacrifice. He embodies the meaning of hearing, as well as the meaning of seeing, before their being joined by way of a subject and an object. The *Wörterbuch der ägyptischen Sprache* lists the meanings of the ancient Egyptian transliteration of *dng* as: a bad property of the ear, an edible plant, a dwarf, a piece of clothing. Someone who assumes that duration is a universal is liable to read any evidence of the non-universal as malfunction. But the notion of an ear as having a "bad property" is like the notion of a womb as "hysterical". The *dng* dwarf, as a "bad property of the ear", effectively describes the nature of the transformation undergone by the victim of the sacrifice. From the point of view of duration, the transformations of the Word may appear to malform the victim and to render sensations excruciating and incomprehensible. But the act of sacrifice is one that denies duration any claim to universal application.

Notes

1. The swaddled stone, like the residual bones of the desert camel, belong to the same order of ritual objects as does the rib extracted from Adam. They represent the significance of the relic—as a means by which the dead can transform into the living.

2. Pythagoras' insight into the mathematical significance contained in terrestrial dissonance—that it "contains" the music of the spheres—is emblemised by the *wadjet* eyes on Bes' cloak.

3. Contact barriers do not exist in nature, and they cannot be directly observed. Altars have to be wrought as objects of human artifice in order to realise the disjunctive transforming powers of the contact barrier as a structure of inspiration.

4. Maspero (1893: 430) thinks this isle to be the isle of "the doubles"—possibly the isle of the *ka-w* (or imaginary twins), on which an eponymous shipwrecked sailor is beached. On this isle, at the verge of the world, fabulous semi-divine beings exist, who are of a liminal nature, one such being the serpent made of precious substances who speaks with a human tongue. This liminal site is associated with things that are wrought or made by craftsmen, a place of art. Maspero (1893: 431) associates the *dng* to Bes, who is also a god of the limen.

5. Khepri's relation to the sun is echoed in mythic thought in other parts of Africa. In a certain Rwandan myth, pygmy courtiers of the sacred king wear an emblem of the forge on their tobacco pouches. Some of them "were in charge of maintaining the sacred fire", which was kept alive throughout the king's life (Heusch, 2000: 52).

6. Goedicke writes that the *dng* dance was performed for the body of the king in its official and cult aspect and not for the body of the king in its human aspect (Dasen, 1993: 133).

7. "In many instances Egyptian religious texts and representations appear contradictory until the cyclic concept of the renewal of life through the cooperation and fusion of opposites is understood. In this fusion, the two widely separated geographic points of West and East, the sunset and sunrise mountains of Manu and Bakhu, become identified and joined, both in thought and in image. From geographic opposites they become associated symbols of the mysterious achievement of divine purpose. The antiquity of this concept is evinced by the rayed sun disk in its positions of descent and ascent placed on either side of the two joined mountains of the horizon" (Rambova, 1957: 30).

8. In any act of Becoming there must be loss, if only of a former state. What Spinoza calls thinking by way of modes (as opposed to thinking by way of attributes) is characterised by the presence of loss—of Becoming as a mutation that activates ideas of memory and history as a means to modify the shock of loss.

9. By way of sound, he is informative about the role of the Holy Spirit, or Word, in the process of creation.

20

*The role of concealment
in the disclosures of time*

Lévi-Strauss (1958: 184) describes the transformation by which "dying" myths are once more reinvigorated in terms of the model of a pin-hole that increases the intensity of light-rays that pass through it by means of an inversion of the light-rays (see chapter 16). Bion (1980: 15) finds a model for transformation in the transference in the way in which the facets of a diamond refract light-rays. When placed within the context of the becoming of "O", these optic models of inversion and refraction describe the sense of hiatus and change in direction that characterise catastrophic change. The parallel between these structures in imaginative transformation and in the transformatory structure of the eye is striking.

In its optical behaviour the eye is essentially like a *camera obscura*. In order for a luminous point to be seen distinctly, the light diverging from it must be refracted by the media of the eye and thereby converged at some point of the retina. On the surface of this membrane a real optical image is projected of the external objects in view, which is inverted and very much reduced in size. [Helmholtz, in Southall, 1962: 91]

Conceivably, structures in imaginative transformation bring into being the transformatory structure of the eye. The body of Shakespeare's non-existent king beneath the water's surface, like some nucleus of the imagination within the eye, is comparable to Lévi-Strauss's "pin-hole", or to the points of refraction on Bion's diamond.[1]

Imaginative space, indistinguishable from the objects it contains, is bound up with catastrophic change. The *churinga*—a religious work of art, with the significance of a relic among some of the Australian aborigine people—exists on the threshold in which systems of time originate. It must be kept for most of time concealed in a cave—the cave having the same value as the point of inversion or of refraction in the theories of Lévi-Strauss and Bion.[2] The imperceptibility of the concealed *churinga* is relevant to the ritual potency by which it is accredited with being able to condense all time and narrative into an atemporal conception of the present, nominally a "first moment", which is identical with any, or every, moment. The *churinga* has impact as a gravitational mass because it is capable of drawing into itself the entire expanse of time and narrative. It exemplifies the idea of a transformation that is absolute and yet can be contained: "Containing all space and time" has the same logic in myth as the death–rebirth transformation of the Holy Sepulchre.

In much the same way as the ancient Egyptian priests would have kept certain sacred statues shrouded within the interior of the temple, so at some *intensified* or festive period in the calendar the *churinga* or the ancient Egyptian statue was brought out of the darkness and exhibited. A specific sacred space, characterised by powers related to concealment, is able thus to transform an absolute negation into an absolute plenitude and, in doing so, to reverse the idea of temporal sequence, so that the future rather than the past is thought to originate the present. This is a theory about function in art, as well as in religion. It is relevant to cave art in general. While the rocks that contain the *churinga* undergo the slow transformation of enduring the climatic changes that mark the passing of time, the *churinga* itself, like the sacred king, must undergo a rigorous *celestial* logic (represented by the space within the rocks) in which the temporality, if any, of the music of silence and music that might render it anew is related to the future.

First man, as cosmogram, personifies the dynamic of the *churinga*. Adam himself has little or no sense of history. He has no past, in the sense that he had no ancestors and no parents. He comes into being not as an infant, but as a youth. He cannot reminisce about childhood, because he has no companions and, in any case, he has had no childhood. But he contains all time and space within himself in the unusual form of containing non-existent ancestors, who are his successors—meaning *us*. He can only look in one direction: at a future that presents itself as an act of sacrifice, in which he himself is the victim and in which the disfiguring of his own body, as in the creation of some primordial work of art, gives rise to Eve as the beauty of inspiration. He conceives of the past as an aspect of the future.

Evocative of the refraction of light in Bion's diamond, his body refracts the light of many avatars, each of whom is, in her or his way, a victim of the sacrifice. In the Judeo–Christian tradition, Adam is, among many others, Abraham, Moses, and King David, as well as the many refractions of Christ. And this theme applies to other religious cultures as well. In certain Islamic texts there are traces of ancient pagan cults, in which culture heroes from very distant times take on the guise of later biblical figures (Chelhod, 1954). The Genesis Adam, who appears among these later biblical figures, possibly represents a reworking of some earlier prototype. Some of these pre-Islamic myths, as they are glimpsed in Islamic texts, are not unlike the refraction of images that might occur behind closed eyelids.

In the logic of the sacrifice, any sensory organ can have the capacity to be inverted or refracted or can be a substitute/equivalent for the body of the king.[3] The charisma of the sacrifice depends on idealising quiddity for its own sake: it contracts the object, and the space in which the object exists, into an accretion that can elude thought.[4] It arises from a mutilation of actual flesh and blood.[5]

> We know little about the circumstances of the sacrifice [among the Barma people of Baguirmi—now a part of Chad]. Our informants spoke little about it, as they did about anything which related to the blacksmith, [who conducts the

sacrifice, and] who is incarnated on earth in the figure of the *mbang*, or king. For some of them the sacrifice must have taken place at the beginning of August (the heliacal rising of Sirius), at the time of the inundation, when the river has swallowed all the waters of the world. [Pâques, 1977: 148]

The blaze of the rising sun is the body of the blacksmith, who in working with fire is fire itself, and who has many of the priestly attributes of kingship; and it is also the Chari river, conceived of as a body that has "swallowed all the waters of the world".

The Chari is thought to be a triple person representing the blacksmith as a terrestrial figure. It consists of three tributaries that join at the "neck" (i.e. the genitals) of the person who extends from the north-west to the south-east, and whose head is identified with lake Chad. Everyone in Barma knows that the head of the Chari has been cut off and that the waters of lake Chad emerge from its "neck." The head, *like the blacksmith's anvil*, has fallen to the south, one part at Sarh (Fort-Archambault) and the other at l'Oubangui. [Pâques, 1977: 148]

This is a theory about how time operates as a sign system on the edge of existence (as opposed to the universal linearity of the writing conception of time). An intuition of catastrophe informs the often unaccountable appearance and disappearance of signs. When faced with the problem of part and whole, traditional cosmology tends to generate rituals.

The bell-*kratér* from Ruvo (Deedes, 1935) (see chapter 15) indicates how a Janus-headed body must be sacrificed in order to separate father and son. Initially, the fusion represents the one who conducts the sacrifice and the one who is sacrificed in terms of an atemporality that is a characteristic of the divine king in his heavenly aspect. But in being terrestrial also, the king must bargain with the notion of endings and beginnings in time. He must undergo death and rebirth. A predecessor must die (and in part be eaten) in order that a successor might be initiated. The old year must die so that a new year can be born.

By the Nile, and by the Niger also, the sacrifice of renewal involves the sky as well as the earth. Sirius, a planet whose closeness to the sun can render it imperceptible, separates from the sun and becomes perceptible at the very time at which the inundation of the river regenerates the fields. It appears out of the light of the sun, much as the *churinga* appears out of the darkness of a cave, like a dead son in rebirth who brings its mother alive once more. The heavens, as the unknowable spatial ground out of which the Word manifests itself, by way of Sirius transforms the earth and initiates the new year.[6]

An ivory plate, dating from the time of King Djer, identifies the new year with the king by having him as the falcon-god Horus seated on a *serekh*, an emblem of his palace, and which is possibly a false door portal into the other world. Before him is Sirius, in the form of a cow mother to Horus. Beneath Sirius is an *ahket* determinative, representing the inundation, and the name of Buto, one of the earliest known sites of reference for the heliacal rising (Bomhard, 1999: 48). In another representation, Sirius and Orion, in separate boats, are half-turned towards each other. Sirius as Isis, or the new year, restores life to Orion as Osiris, who is the victim of the sacrifice (ibid.: 24). Similarly, the Ruvo *kratér* shows the god of the new year as stretching out to Hera, as the mother goddess, whom he seeks to appropriate from his father. In the African models, the mother goddess is less an object to be possessed than a representation of the terrestrial appearance of the celestial Word.

The sacrifice of the body of the king—whether as the river (Adam as agriculturist) or as the solar blacksmith (Adam as the blacksmith who understands the mysterious alchemy by which fire becomes music)—is evocative of the rib-extraction myth in Genesis, in which the extracting of the rib marks the rebirth of a solar king. Sirius (or Eve in the legend) separates from the solar radiance and becomes perceptible.

> For better or worse at Maypa they relate this event [the coincidence of the heliacal rising of Sirius and the inundation] to the legend of Moses and the Pharaoh, who on this occasion are the Nabi Dawud (King David is an ancestor of the blacksmiths) and Firuna (the Pharaoh). "Both combatants for some unknown reason were close to the sea at Malya. Dawud divided the waters of the sea, which then closed on the people of Firuna, who were transformed into hippopotami and various fish. . . ."[7] At Bousso, as at Mapling, this event is

connected not with Dawud but with Nabi Nuku (Noah).
When the archangel Djibrila (Gabriel?) had cut down the del
tree, Nuku made the river flow from a large stone in the
south and constructed a large pirogue out of the del tree.
[Pâques, 1977: 148]

Within the diamond body of the king, light-rays refract a series
of transformations. Transforming "the people of Firuna", or the
Pharaoh, into water creatures, is no different, as an organ of the
imagination, from the malign Platonic womb, which converts
cosmos into chaos, or from the sea matrix in which the eyes of a
non-existent king transform into pearls. Paradigms for hysteria
are sometimes used to describe catastrophic change paradigms.

The traditional relation of the blacksmith to music.   A priest-
like figure who works as a blacksmith is one such version of the
sacred king. In pre-Islamic belief, he is an Adam who gives his
fellow men the tools of the forge, the ploughshare, and the
needle (the techniques of agriculture and weaving). He is a
blacksmith and musician, as well as an agriculturist and priest.

> In effect, as Ibn Abbas has claimed, *Adam brought down the
> hammer, the anvil and the pincers from Paradise. . . .* The
> Koran endorses a pre-Islamic belief that iron initially fell
> from the skies. God himself instructed King David to invent
> and to make the first coat of mail. Massoudi affirms the
> celestial origins of agriculture: *when Adam descended from
> Paradise to live on earth he brought with him thirty branches
> from different trees.* Kazwini proposes that the Archangel
> Michael brought down wheat and taught men how to sow and
> harvest it. [Chelhod, 1954: 53]

The Genesis God grants Adam the prerogative to name the
animals:[8] and it is through Adam that man is able to realise the
power of the Word. In Dogon creationism, similarly, the blacksmith brings down the Word from the skies by having descend
the techniques of the forge and of the loom.

> Weaving has the power of the Word. This quasi magical
> power arouses fear in other members of the society. If the
> inseminating power of the Word is less evident in the forge, it
> is because the Word is replaced by the sounds of the ham-

mers. It is curious to observe that the noun *qayn*, meaning blacksmith, when it takes a feminine ending, *qayna*, means a singer or in pre-Islamic Arabia *a fille de joie*. [Chelhod, 1954: 56][9]

The blacksmith is often a companion of the minstrel, and his role in culture gives expression to a sexuality that might otherwise be denied. People avoid and fear him, in part because of his obscenity in speech and behaviour, and in part because he draws pentagrams, which they associate with disaster—in spite of their believing that the five fingers of an opened hand can protect a face against evil.[10] They avoid him because of his close relation to fire, out of which the demons of music are born.[11] And they avoid him because God has set him apart from other men.

Notes

1. An incandescent infant's body, intimating the existence of the future in the transference, can represent the diamond body of the divine king.

2. It is like the dreaming that occurs with closed eye-lids.

3. In the sacrifice, the distinction between substitution and identicality is slight.

4. If I operate Freud's model of secondary function, then these accretions will be thought to consist of beta elements. If I operate Bion's model of the becoming of "O", then the nature of the accretions is more problematic. The theory of beta elements falls away as a residual of Cartesianism.

5. Part objects are negations of actual bodily parts. Confusing the idea in negation of the part object with the concrete conception of bodily parts results in that curious hybrid, the ghost.

6. The Dogon provide an architectonic for this conception of time in a granary structure that functions as a gnomon and registers time by way of the movement of the sun across the skies. There is a creative ease in this linking of the measure of the solar body with the measure of the harvest.

7. The transformation of historical legend—the Mosaic crossing of the red sea—into myth. Moses as the high priest, representing God, creates the animals by sacrificing the pharaoh as the divine king. A similar link between the animals and naming occurs in relation to the Genesis account of the sacrifice of Adam.

8. The idea of the Word is similar in the Judeo-Christian and the Dogon traditions.

9. Note the sound similarities between *qayn* and Kanté, a well-known name among West African blacksmiths. "By the fig-tree were the two

houses of *Kantenumu*, blacksmiths whose name was Kanté. When I was a child, I feared to pass this fig-tree at dusk, thinking it to be the place where there were sorcerers and Dijons" (Kante, 1993: 11). Also note the sound similarity between qayn and Tubal-cain, a blacksmith descendant of Adam who is a brother to a musician. "And Lamech took unto him two wives: the name of the one was Adah, and the name of the other Zillah. And Adah bare Jabal: he was the father of such as dwell in tents, and of such as have cattle. And his brother's name was Jubal: he was the father of all such as handle the harp and organ. And Zillah, she also bare Tubal-cain, an instructor of every artificer in brass and iron" (Genesis 4: 19–22) (see also Pâques, 1977: 11).

10. He practises sacred geometry, as does Plato's demiurge.

11. Similarly in Pythagoreanism the tapping of a bronze surface releases the sound of the lunar demon within the bronze. The lunar demon, trapped within the bronze, is in exile from its rightful congregation in the music of the spheres.

21

Placenta & womb as means of creation

> Our informants told us that all signs are signs of the
> anvil. The blacksmith, as master of initiation, is master
> of the sign.
>
> Dieterlen & Cissé, 1972: 13

Throughout much of Africa the heavens are the source of the culture of the sign.[1] Among the Minyanka people, the signs derive from the placenta of the sky-god responsible for all creation (Jespers, 1976: 117). The burial in sacks of altar-fetishes, on which are marked signs, and the burial of actual placentas in the ground ritually correspond to the descent of the heavenly signs. The placenta "is the alter ego of the new-born. It is the silent witness of the first words uttered *in utero* by the individual and, by analogy, of the first words registered in the celestial placenta. It contains the signs which constitute the first creation" (Jespers, 1979: 82). Out of it "the universe was created" (Jespers, 1976: 117). Its being buried in a jar, which in turn is buried in the earth, is token of its being a death-and-resurrection object.

In order that sign systems should have the value of icons, there has to be some catastrophic transition between cosmological domains. The creation of the aesthetic or sacred space of the icon requires an instrumentality, or *yantra*, which uses "interruption" as a means to intensify the light-rays of thought and feeling (in terms of optics, the interruption is Lévi-Strauss's "inversion" or Bion's "refraction"). In traditional cosmology, the transition by which the aniconic permeates the perceptible often takes the form of a horizon crossing. The placenta is like a meteor that has entered the atmosphere of ancient Egypt. It is the iron of pre-Islamic belief which "initially fell from the skies" (Chelhod, 1954: 53) (see chapter 20). In its being buried, the placenta releases into its subterranean place *the qualities that the subterranean place might acquire it if were to ascend into the sky*. A counterpart for the placenta in the burial rite of death and regeneration is the solar dragon of Vedic myth, who exists within the primeval mound, and who must be slain in order to initiate the rising of the sun.

The blind one-time hunter Ogotemmêli informed Marcel Griaule (1948) that among the Dogon people the means that creates signs, which the Dogon think of as the Word, had to descend three times from the heavens. Each of the Word's descents translates into one of the dimensions that the craftsman requires.

> The first Word gives rise to a simple and archaic technique, which consists of a fibre that flows in a serpentine line and in a single dimension. The second Word gives rise to an act of weaving, which entails a second dimension. The third Word involves three dimensions. It gives rise to a cylinder covered in copper: the drum. [Griaule, 1948: 71–72]

The first Word.   If placenta is agent for the sign that appears in acts of geomantic divination as an equivalence for the act of cosmic creation itself, then womb is agent for the sacrifice, for the death-in-life significance of being a terrestrial creature, who may die in being born. The menstruation of the womb concretely brings out its likeness to the act of sacrifice. A placenta must take on the role of the object of sacrifice, if a newborn is not to die in the act of birth.

Certain myths touch on the fear aroused by menstruation. In one myth, blood flows from mother earth. As a rationalisation of dread, the myth recounts how mother-earth has been violated by her husband, the sky-god Amma, and how, on another occasion, she is violated by a son born of the father's act of rape. The son—an animal of some kind (jackal or fox or hyena), with many names (Ogo and Yourougou being among them)—steals a fragment of its own birth placenta and makes the earth out of it, by which act it renders the earth arid.

Certain water spirits, called the Nommo, attempt to repair mother-earth (who is their mother also) by descending from the sky and by having certain fibres descend with them. Out of the fibres they make a skirt for the earth-mother—and the fibres absorb her flowing blood. The fibres, in their sky descent, assume the shapes of helix, spiral, circle, or the luminous meander of river waters, evocative "of whirlpools turning in water or air, of the undulating of serpents and of the gyrating of the eight spirals which move around the sun" (Griaule, 1948: 26). That which is made, and that out of which the making is made, are aspects of the Word.

The second Word.   The descent of the second Word entails a complicated sub-plot, concerning the creation of the eight ancestors of mankind. Lébé, the seventh ancestor, is "master of the Word". In Ogotemmêli's account of the second descent, the Word transforms the jaws of Lébé into a loom, so that in acts of biting and speaking he is able to expectorate thread and to weave speech into existence. Acts of weaving and of making the objects of culture are strongly compared to jaw movements in talk and eating. In the order of time, the weaver has precedence over the blacksmith, the musician, and the tiller of land. "The sign bears witness to the divine word at the stage of creation. Weaving symbolises the Word at the oral stage, as it is revealed to men. It is said that *weaving speaks the mind* or that *the noise or voice of the weaving is the Word*" (Dieterlen & Cissé, 1972: 195). In some myths, Lébé, who is murdered or sacrificed, is resurrected in the form of a serpent, who is related to agrarian rites and rites of harvest. Nightly, he slides in the form of a serpent to the house of the Hogon, or high priest of the Dogon, and imbues the (sleeping?) Hogon with chthonic authority by licking him from tip to toe.

The third Word. In *Le Renard pâle* (1965), Griaule and Dieterlen do not follow Ogotemmêli's narrative in describing the three descents of the Word. They concentrate their attention on the descent of the third Word. In particular, they attempt to show how the theme of celestial descent is related to the inseparable relationship of sacrifice and creation—creation being represented in this case by the signs that arise through acts of divination.

Amma, the first God, sacrifices his beloved son, Nommo *anagonno*, and out of Nommo's body creates a celestial ark— which in some versions of the myth takes the form of a celestial forge, or granary. The ark brings to earth, as a realisation of the wrought, the idea of culture itself. By way of acts of making, mankind is able to transfigure the meaning of divinatory signs. Working with clay, wood, or metal necessarily involves some relationship with the sky-god.

The first drum is the skull of Nommo. The institution of the sacrifice, signifying death, and the institution of divination (the arising of signs as evidence of a returning plenitude), provide the space of embodiment, and embodiment itself, with a grammar. This is a way of describing the nature of the icon or *yantra*. The African sculptor, or a maker, or constructor in general, equates the divine body with the stuffs with which he works— and in this way he can release the very *isness* of the material, or equate void with body as charismatic absence, by allowing the void to generate the plane surface. Music discloses more clearly than the other arts such a structuring of planes about a void.

Initially, the signs, as manifestations of the unpredictable, arise out of "nothing" (Dieterlen & Cissé, 1972: 179). "Creationist myths among the [*neighbouring*] Bambara involve a philosophy of Being in which the universe is evolved from the void, from nothing, from /u" (Dieterlen, 1950: 28). "The sign zero (*fu*) represents the beginnings of creation and the origins of all things" (ibid.: 93). An anvil descends from the sky with the metaphysical authority of the sacred king's body, or of the celestial placenta.[2] It is a repository for all the signs.

A visitor to Dogon country will observe, close to the village of Sanga, how the place of circumcision—a site of pain and dread—is next to a cliff on which many red and white signs are marked. A cave in the cliff contains a sistrum and other musical instruments. Musicians play these instruments during the circumcision. Circumcision and music are related by means of the blacksmith, who carries out the circumcision, and his twin, who is the musician. Both of them are avatars of the sacred king.

Music, being among the more potent of sign systems, carries within itself, often in a veiled form, the presence of catastrophe. (At one time the Dogon made musical instruments out of the bones and skins of animals that had been sacrificed.) The *twin : contact barrier : twin* triad implies a triad in which *Holy Spirit* or *the spirit of music* replaces *contact barrier*. In Ovid's *Metamorphosis*, the sun-god Apollo orders the flaying of Marsyas, a flute-player who thinks to rival Apollo. Here we have *Apollo : flute playing : Marsyas* as representing the triad. Ogotemmêli has a myth in which the pain of circumcision is translated into an ascending of the foreskin of the victim in the form of a lizard that unites with the sun (Griaule, 1948: 162–163). In the Apollo legend, by day the heavens, in the form of the sun, transform harmony into dissonance. Apollo keeps the art of music to himself and relegates the dissonance of pain and screaming to Marsyas; he possibly appropriates Marsyas's skin.

In *Le renard pâle* Griaule and Dieterlen relate the sacrifice to the coming into existence of the anvil as the repository of signs and the coming into existence of the instruments of music.[3] In redeeming the world,[4] "Amma sacrifices Nommo, divides his body into pieces and throws them out of the sky in order to purify space and Earth" (Dieterlen, in Alexandre, 1972: 44). The celestial blacksmith and the musician are formed as twins out of the body of Nommo *anagonno*.

> He made the blacksmith from Nommo's umbilical cord (the part which had remained attached to the placenta), and from blood which had flowed from the cord and from Nommo's penis, which had been severed at the same time. He created

the musician out of the placenta and from the sacrificial
blood taken from Nommo's cut throat ... (because of their
mixed blood, blacksmiths and musicians are forever denied
the right to marry out of caste). The act of sacrifice emptied
the penis and testicles of Nommo of a "harvest" consisting of
the four elements. The blacksmith, in receiving the "harvest",
also received a part of one of Nommo's arms, emptied of its
marrow and transformed into a hammer, containing cereal
grains. After the descent of the ark (which carried with it the
Word), Amma ordered the blacksmith to descend first—by
way of his right as twin—using his sexual organs as a support. The blacksmith placed his two arms in his two testicles
and his legs into the length of his penis. On landing, these
elements transformed into his penis as the furnace pipe and
his testicles as the bellows of the forge. [Griaule & Dieterlen,
1965: 375–378]

The musician, who carries Nommo's skull, makes the first drum
out of his skull. The drum is a variant on Adam's rib, or the
buried sacred relics of divine kings, or, more signally, the armature of a cranial space, in which there is pulse, and in which
perception might occur, before the development of an optic or
auditory equipment. The sonority of the drum authenticates its
celestial origins, so that it speaks with the Word. "The mythic
prototype of the *tabale* drum was made of copper, a primordial
metal whose 'vibration' assimilates it to the vibration of light, of
sound, of water and of the Word" (Pâques, 1954: 106). (Kings
and chiefs alone have access to the *tabale* drum.) The sonority of
the drum binds the third Word to the meanders of luminous
water, and to the circling in a void, which typify the appearance
of the first Word.

There is a stage during the making of lutes when the identification of the lute's frame with the body of the god, during the
time of death and resurrection, entails that the frame of the lute
be buried for three days and then dug up.[5] The lute-player relies
on the inspiration of the Word to activate the potency of the four
different types of wood from which he makes the instrument,
each one of which has a separate mythological resonance and is
related in a different way to the theme of regeneration; each one
of which has a particular relationship to the four elements and

to the four orients. The lute is a form of ear–mouth. Through its powers of orientation, it generates sounds that reach to the ends of the cosmos. It is microcosm as macrocosm; and as its music unfolds, it makes the idea of magnitude disappear.

As the lute-player among the Dogon was about to play, he was heard to whisper into the body of his instrument, *Today is your day, and this is what I say to you—organise the world!* [Griaule & Dieterlen, 1950: 224]

Notes

1. In the ancient Egyptian Pyramid texts (Faulkner, 1969) and else-where, hieroglyphs describe rites that are situated in the heavens. But are they themselves celestial in origin?—only to the extent to which they are part of a pan-African commitment to sign-making. Hieroglyphs are apt representations for the ancient Greek hesitation as to whether marks should be more valued as signs or as writing. It is not clear whether they belong to sign thinking or to the writing conception.

2. A celestial object touches the earth and transforms it, but not neces-sarily with a benign or peaceful outcome. Similarly, the footsteps of Vishnu or of the Buddha were thought to have this potent and disturbing effect. "The placentas of mothers in miscarriage are placed high in the branches of a certain tree to protect the community from impurity" (Dieterlen & Cissé, 1972: 44 *n*2)

3. The circle of divination appears to be the portal through which music, as well as signs, arise from the nether-world, except that by the logic of this kind of container the nether-world is a residence in the sky.

4. The sacrifice of Nommo *anagonno* reverses the celestial–terrestrial transformation of the Pythagorean legend of the smithy, since here the sacrifice, or dissonance, occurs in the sky and is then transformed into a means of consonance on earth.

5. In it being buried, the lute frame is comparable to the placenta in its role as "silent witness of the first words uttered *in utero* by the indi-vidual" (Jespers, 1979: 82). The lute frame, like the placenta, in taking on death (the significance of being buried), authenticates the "resurrection" of birth. The music of the newborn fills the cosmos like the sound of a lute, in an alleluia at having survived a journey through the valley of death.

22

Concerning axiality & threshold

In an ancient Brahminical tradition, the making of
diagrams representing a deity and his forces, or groups
of divinities, remains the best way to represent the
invisible universe of the forces that govern the cosmos.
These "organised" representations of the divine universe
are still widely used in India on many occasions, ritual
and other—to invoke the deity, to expel evil spirits, to
reconcile wandering souls, or to ask a favour of the
celestial powers. They are still attested today by the
ritual designs drawn on the ground before their houses
by the women in the Indian countryside. These ritual
diagrams are in fact a sort of writing to communicate
with the deities, and perhaps derive their origin from
magic signs.

Frédéric, 1995: 33

The writing conception disavows any creationist assumption concerning creation and the sacrifice, or concerning the emergence of plenitude from a negation in plenitude. Its idea of time is of an indefinite linearity, in which the universe is like a blank scroll on which some imaginary calligrapher unfolds the script of time.

In sign-system thinking, conceptions of time are quite different. Out of the cataclysm of the void (which in rite is the act of sacrifice), random signs form into sequences, which can be as varied in type as are forms in music. Initially the sign-indicators of temporality are more inclined to be associated with the future than the present or the past. Often there is cataclysm; and then some attempt to re-establish axiality after cataclysm.

* * *

In the religions (broadly speaking) of Asia, image-cult is less qualified and less complicated than in the religions of the West. The image, whether as a carving or as a temple, appears to be of greater moment than the text. The iconography of the forms of life known as Hinduism and Buddhism vividly engage the perceptions of the observer, even though the sacred commentaries on these images have been known to be opaque.

The meaning of the image lies not in its spatiality, let alone its visuality. Although it communicates by way of the visual, its appeal lies elsewhere: in its communication of time as an icon of eternity. Paul Mus has observed that time is "the favoured symbolic object of all Indian architecture" (1935: 160), even though the temples to which Mus primarily refers are armatures in three-dimensional space, often consisting of great mass. How can time, rather than spatiality, be the motive that brings them into existence?

This may be, in part, because of their frequent identification with the sun as a chariot, which marks out time by its progress across the skies. In the traditional cosmology of India, the sun has two functions. As agent for catastrophic change, it is a terrible "eye", which blinds anyone who looks into it.[1] When it reaches the zenith of its diurnal course, it is a "fifth point" (see below) which presents itself as a sun-door, or limen, that is virtually impossible to cross (Coomaraswamy, 1939).[2] The threshold of the sun-door marks a point of transition between time and eternity: its relation to temporality as sequence could not be more contingent. The coincidence of sun and zenith is an imaginative as well as an actual fact; it is timeless (the sun is suspended in the midday sky, as though forever), and yet it is so momentary that it might pass unnoticed. This is a religious understanding of the catastrophic-change theory.

By way of catastrophic change, the sun discloses that time is important *because all forms of time,* in retrieving order from cataclysm, *are systems of axiality.* Time is an instrument of value in relation to a certain specific end, which is to restore a negation in cosmos into a cosmos in plenitude. On the threshold of catastrophic change (which men imitate in conducting an act of sacrifice), the sun brings into being the *axis mundi*—in the form of light-rays. And by way of the *axis mundi*, it activates geometric forms, notably the wheel and the labyrinth. Out of geometric forms arise the multiple schemas of time.

In its diurnal progress, the sun, in drawing a shape that is like the segment of a wheel, is evocative of "the women in the Indian countryside" who draw ritual designs "on the ground before their houses" (Frédéric, 1995: 33). By its articulating of time, the sun daily creates a *mandala* in the heavens. Fundamentally, the wheel that the instrument of light draws in the sky is an agent for the presence of an *axis mundi*.

Fifth point. At the "centre" of a space filled by a body to be orientated to four points is a fifth point, which is either above, or beneath, the four horizontal points—as a zenith or a nadir. By way of the fifth point, there occur transformations in dimensionality. The fifth point can take the form of a threshold that transforms from point into the line of the *axis mundi*—a vertical in opposition to the horizontal plane, that is yet in creative alliance with the four points on the horizontal plane. An actual object, such as a sacrificial post, can represent it as a verticality. In creationist sequence, the *axis mundi* generates the horizontal of four points, possibly as eyes and ears within a cranial structure, or as four orients that arms and legs, when extended, can indicate. Such is one of the means by which time, initially conceived of in absolute terms as continuity or interruption, transfigures into space. Duration *becomes* extension.

A certain Vedic text interrogates the *axis mundi* about its relation to time.[3] "Wherein what hath been and shall be, and all worlds are instant, tell me thou of that pillar (*skambha, axis mundi*), what it may be" (Coomaraswamy, 1947: 10). As a concept of the imagination, the *axis mundi* represents the cosmos in its aspect of negation as well as plenitude; in its vertical descent, it is a beam of darkness as well as a beam of light. Its dual nature indicates how varied types of sequentiality have come into being. It is both solid and void; it is life when faced by death, or death when faced by regeneration; and it is never quite free from the accusation of murder. As *nothing* as well as *everything*, it articulates the idea of the sacrifice as the dynamic of sacred space.[4]

> It is not just that it marks the centre, and that it rises up and dominates the stupa in the form of a staff bearing parasols: the entire masonry which surrounds and encloses it, is explained by it, and constitutes no more than—in a single word—its envelope. [Mus, 1935: 121]

Plato and the theme of duration as a universal. Occidental thought often postulates the universality of duration. Descartes's belief that truth must be "distinct" (or available for location) as well as "clear" depends on this assumption. If existences that were not durational were to exist, there would be no necessity to relate truth to location. Truth could be "clear" (perceptible or felt) without having to be "distinct". By an elaboration on this position, feelings, perceptions, or sensations, which cannot be placed in context, are assumed to be delusional: and by this belief originates a tradition in psychiatry, in which "locating" feelings, perceptions, or sensations is essential to their being thought true.[5]

The seventeenth century, as an age of great explorers, is also an age of great anatomists: discovering the location of things postulates a universe in which things have locations. It presumes that in some pristine state of existence, things have their proper place; and it expels the idea of an untidy or wayward Holy Spirit into the wilderness. Mankind, in the form of Adam the gardener, acquired as a part of its inheritance an immaculate garden.[6] Eve, and her first-born, the serpent as a devilish mess-making first-born, have to carry the blame that is often apportioned to the confusions of creativity.

Existences that can be mapped are "real" existences, and they are analogous in their topography to bodies. Communication fails if this does not occur. Bion's "disorder of thought" results; or, possibly, some collapse in what Freud called secondary process. In secondary process, the object of enquiry is the "other": it is that which is *there*, in one place, awaiting to be observed, endorsing the observer's intuition concerning the existence of the axiality, within and without the self, and without which the ego of the observer would founder. But dual systems of this kind are only dual seemingly, as Lévi-Strauss (1956) has observed. The alternation between subject and object depends on a third element: a zero function that is a variable without content and is crucial to the enabling of reciprocity between subject and object, as well as to the annihilation of any obsessional model on which they might depend. There is the becoming of "O", a sometimes imperceptible form of catastrophic change. In the traditional cosmology of India, zero function is the sacrificial act out of which time arises. In terms of signs, it is the icon by which the non-durational translates into systems of duration by means of cataclysm. Art attempts to modify the cataclysmic effect of this eruption into time.

In Platonism, zero function is largely imperceptible, or it is present as a numinous "One", which endows the existence of numbers, whether or not in sequence, with the qualities of a sacred mystery. The One has the authority to determine conceptions of time; and it is for this reason that the narrator of the *Timaeus* is able to assert that time is an icon for eternity (icon equalling zero). Plato's thought exists on the cusp between sign–system thinking and the writing conception. He is fascinated by the kind of thinking that gives rise to the icon, but he also distrusts it: possibly, he intuited some cognate relation between the icon and cataclysm. It is as though he recognised that the icon bore witness to its source in some process in which all traces of duration must disappear. He anticipates the later more intransigent commitment of the West to the cult of duration, at the expense of the sign–system understanding of the icon.

Axis mundi. Forked lightning splits the night skies; and out of this splitting, opposed interpretations of the sacrifice arise. One interpretation, which is "masculine", describes the sacrificial dismemberment in terms of "riddles", which are inversions of the imaginative. The Janus-head in the Ruvo *kratér* is one example of the enigmatic and fused nature of the riddle; the Oedipal sphinx is another. Fundamentally, all riddles communicate different aspects of the same concrete equation, in which there is no distinction made between the one who performs the sacrifice and the one who is sacrificed. Another interpretation is "feminine". It attempts to modulate dread of the sacrifice by retrieving axiality from the moment of disintegration, often by way of a pattern, the *kolam* drawn by women at first light, at the beginning of the year, a prototype of the idea of the "image in form".[7]

Although Vespasian man lies with limbs outstretched within a sacred circle, an indeterminate "zero" space (the Holy Spirit?) can divide the sacred circle into two circles (much as the horizon daily separates the heavens from the earth). One circle is the place of the sacrifice, the other is the place of divination. A "masculine" interpretation draws attention to the iconography of the sacrifice, while a "feminine" interpretation draws attention to an iconography of divination, in which the future, as a void radiating the meaning of the sacrifice, speaks to the present. This is a way of describing the difference between the threshold (the gap) and the geometric forms, which arise from the threshold and which retrieve some means of axiality.

The feminine act of modulating terror—for instance, by drawing *kolams*—is able to elucidate the significance of the "riddle" thinking of the masculine interpretation, which emphasises initiation as an examination in which you are bound to fail. In ancient Greek legend, Daedalus creates a labyrinth (or geometric form) for Ariadne. It personifies and contains catastrophic change in the form of a solar bull. But the labyrinth is a net that must break: the solar power that it fails to hold escapes; and Daedalus must be the horrified witness to the solar sacrifice of his son, Icarus. On other occasions, in the same nucleus of myths, the feminine interpretation is more noticeable. Ariadne, as Hera, in her play with the baby Dionysus (who might be an avatar for Icarus), creates a pattern that can arrest the enactment of fall. Her crane-dance shadows forth the shape of the labyrinth through dance steps, and her beauty in dance expands and transfigures the enigmatic "riddle"-like symbolism of the labyrinth. She traces out the shape of the *orchestra*, which is an area of staging situated before an actual stage, a space on which the enactment of drama was eventually to depend. In providing Theseus with a clue that leads him through the complexity of the labyrinth, she reveals how the labyrinth symbolises the overcoming of impediment, as well as the nature of impediment: it is sacrifice as an act to be overcome rather than an act to be capitulated to.

In the "masculine" interpretation, the concept of time is an outcome of the sacrifice. Continuity and sequence exist for only one purpose: to disclose the presence of the discontinuity that is fundamental to the meaning of the sacrifice. The solar bull in Ariadne's heart is the infant Dionysus, who from the "masculine" viewpoint must be butchered and cannibalised, in order to transform a cosmos in negation into a cosmos in plenitude.

As *existence itself*, the becoming of "O" cannot be represented, and would seem to have no place in the topographical picture of reality as other than a somewhat spectral zero function. But although it appears to be irrelevant to a world conceived of as made up of distinctive activities, it is in effect subversive of any notion of the Cartesian "distinct".

That time schemes might be signs arising out of a void exists in opposition to the belief that everything must exist in linear time. The fifth point "out there" is the solar threshold patterning (which may be one of the original and literal meanings of *solar plexus*): but it is also the solar plexus or centre in everyone. Only the artistry or craftsmanship of the "feminine" interpretation will retrieve axiality from the void. In terms of the human body, the fifth point as void–centre can occur in the actual guts, or in the heart, or in the head, or in the absence of place in which there is sensation (the imaginary limb of referred pain), or in other possible bodily locations.

In the traditional cosmology, the fifth point, or the power of the sun to induce catastrophic change, is identifiable with some combined representation of head–stomach; and the head–stomach, in turn, is identifiable, as a symbol, with the sun as the portal to catastrophic change. The fifth point can be a head under threat from decapitation, the bowels, the womb, the navel/umbilical cord (which can be associated with space as a variable capable of expansion[8]) or the genitals of either sex. These "centres of being" perform a zero function; and by them the void realises itself as a system of signs. The sun, as agent for catastrophic change, is the future speaking to the present.

Refractors of the imaginative.   In Dahomey, Bernard Maupoil (1943: 186 et seq.) came across certain divination tablets, representing the macrocosm. Four sculpted heads on each divination tablet faced a different orient. Maupoil related these multiple heads to a Dahomey myth concerning a goat with four eyes, a victim of the sacrifice, with whom the king of Ife was identified. The heads have the meaning of eyes; and the eyes, in turn, are related to the diviner's assumption that the future can release signs or portents into the present. The future, like a light beam, passes through the four head–eyes. They are jewel-like structures, and they increase the intensity of the light-rays that pass through them by means of refraction.[9]

Myth is one of the ways by which the imagination speaks: and in myth, if not in actuality, it is possible to assert that the future can speak to the present. The four head–eyes are refractors of the imaginative, possibly forms of eye and ear that exist before the foetal eyes and ears have come into being. They are a means by which the "unthinkable" can become present in sensation by way of the concept of regeneration.

In terms of traditional cosmology, the four head–eyes support the throne of the divine king. By them, the king is raised to the sun and confirmed in his identification with the dual power of the sun, in that he is able to initiate catastrophic change, as well as to initiate the calendar of his people.

Each of the faces on the four sides of the Bayon towers (*at Angkor, in Cambodia*) look towards a cardinal point. They were thought to represent the god Brahma, who is generally sculpted with four faces. But a Chinese envoy, who visited Angkor in 1296, informs us that the heads were then five in number, the middle one being covered in gold. Louis Finot— believing that the Bayon was a Hindu temple dedicated to Shiva—formulated the theory that the towers were enor-

mous *lingas* sculptured with heads. But the discovery of a
pediment representing Lokeshvara indicated that the original character of the Bayon was Buddhist. Paul Mus described
the sculpted faces as representing a "royal power blessing the
four quarters of the country". Brahma, Shiva or Lokeshvara
would have served equally well to express this abstract idea.
[Cœdès, 1943: 137–139]

The towers, which were thought to have been embellished by
the *four* heads of Brahma, turn out—according to the Chinese
envoy of 1296—to have been towers embellished by *five* Shiva
heads, the top head having disappeared (Cœdès, 1943: 138).
Similarly a catalogue to the museum at Sarnath—as referred to
by Paul Mus (1935: 147)—describes as "lost" "the wheel which
once surmounted the Sarnath pillar". Mus does not see this loss
as a matter of chance;[10] it is relevant to his thesis that time is
the motive for the sacred art of India. The "loss" indeed is a way
of symbolising the power of negation-in-plenitude of the fifth
point, a power particularly related to Shiva. The Bayon towers
and the Sarnath pillar belong to the same order of mythic
reality as the sacrificial post or the Shiva linga. The Bayon
towers are crowned by five heads (one of which is missing). The
Sarnath pillar is crowned by four lions (heads, manes, and part
bodies), at right angles to each other, with a missing (royal?)
wheel above the four gazes. Linking the four heads on the
Bayon towers and the four lions on the Sarnath pillar informs
the possibility that these four objects are supports for the king's
throne, which is present as an absence. The missing wheel, an
emblem for divine royalty, circles the king's head like a halo: the
sun as background to the king's head, or the beam of light that
relates the infant to the celestial realm by way of its fontanel,
gives the newborn its nimbus or halo.

Mus observes that the spatiality of Indian iconism exists as
a means for a regeneration, which manifests itself through time,
through a "music" that is temporality as the axial that modu-
lates sound, even though this act of regeneration is inimical to
any idea of sequence. "Our [Sarnath] pillar is a symbol of great
significance. Does it not give tangible appearance to the idea of
time?" (Mus, 1935: 157). "The Sarnath pillar is an image of the
fabulous cosmic *skambha* (or *axis mundi*) which sustains the

earth and the earth during the time of their separation. . . . It supports all the dimensions of space as well as the sky" (ibid.: 153). Mus proposes that all Indian architecture *engenders a multiplication of forms in space in order to articulate the idea of periodicity* (ibid.: 160). "The same metaphysic which conceives each point of the world as an image of the world" (ibid.: 157) could not fail to make each instance of time a macrocosmic image of periodicity.

The Sarnath pillar is a paradigm constituted of five points, in which the fifth point represents the conjunction of either Sun–zenith or of Venus–zenith (Venus as a five-pointed star). "In its conception of the four cardinal points, India has never forgotten the fifth point: better still, it has assigned to it the most important role" (ibid.: 144), even when the fifth point, as generator of the imagination, has the power of presence which characterises the absent object.

An initiate king is the new year in all its promise. His followers raise him to the sun by means of various supports, or he is situated on a pillar or mountain. But in his identification with the fifth point, with the power of the sun at its zenith, he is in touch with the act of catastrophic change, which initiates systems of time. He becomes the sacrifice by which a new king is initiated.

He is comparable to a certain conception of deity, whose absolute powers create the cosmos as a negation, or an absence in plenitude. Brahma, or Plato's demiurge in the *Timaeus*, are examples of such creators of cosmic negation, and it is perhaps typical of them that they should be fragile, to the point of being non-existent personalities. Brahma is little more than a "threshold" (Biardeau, 1981: 68), and Plato's demiurge, in dividing up the *anima mundi*, is an actor without character. The act of creation absorbs whatever personality these gods might have, and little remains of them, except the act of making (which they initiate and which reifies in the form of a pattern out of the act of making).

An ancient text on architecture (the *Brhat-Samhita*) indicates that "an unbroken series of sages" has transmitted knowledge of architecture (*vastu*) from the time of Brahma (Kramrisch, 1946: 10–12). Among these sages are astronomers and astrologers, as well as architects and priests. Equating temple with cosmos entails equating temple with the heavens. "The diagram of the temple and the images carved on its walls allocate a place to the regents of the planets and the stars, who regulate the measurements of the whole building. They regulate, too, the life of the donor and the age of the temple" (ibid.).

The hanged man.   Often, travellers in South India may come across effigies of a man hanged by the neck from the highest point on the scaffolding of incomplete buildings. Sacrificial victims, when slaughtered, vouchsafe the sacrality of the building by being buried in the foundations of a building: they represent an identification of the limbs of Prajâpati, the dismembered first man, with the separate bricks of the sacrificial fire altar; and the idea of some sacrificial victim is usually included in the drawing of temple ground plans.[11] But the effigy of the hanged man is not of a buried figure; it exists between heaven and earth, betwixt and between, on the upper level of a roofless building, whose scaffolding poles jut up into the skies. The building is roofless—in other words, without a head—and to this extent it is like the hanged man. But the hanged man is not exactly like the roofless building, because someone has provided him with a substitute head, in place of the head that is missing. The substitute head takes in the form of a cooking pot. This situation raises the possibility that if the cooking pot stands for the head, or a bodily part, of somebody other than the hanged man, then the someone other must also be a headless corpse, and there must exist at least two decapitated and possibly mutilated bodies. A spectrum opens up of bodies without heads, or of bodies with many heads—or of heads without bodies: a theme of profound implication in the mythology of ancient India. Alternations between heads and bodies of this kind are pointers in traditional cosmology to the nature of time, insofar as time is related to the heavens, and to the idea of the horizon, rather than to the earth.

In traditional cosmology, the incomplete, whether as building or rite, is like the undifferentiated: it is a source for anxiety and a stimulus to creative endeavour. It intimates the void.

Primal creation is always now and always a beginning. At any time, the god of negation might interrupt the creation of a cosmos in plenitude. The effigy of the hanged man is an emblem for an incomplete state—which may never be completed. In this view of culture, constructed objects are not additions to an ongoing situation: they are evidence of a cosmos that is about to begin. There is no accretion; everything is first time. For this very reason, at the beginning of Genesis, God is not allowed the satisfaction of failing, of having an experience of a task that is beyond his powers. His act of creation has to be complete, as well as perfect. Otherwise, a horizon might fail to materialise; and sky and earth would extend into each other.

The reciprocity of fifth point with the other four points is one of absence and presence. If one disappears, then the other appears. The fifth point is anywhere or nowhere: but when it takes spatial form, it can be a vertical line, which travels through the horizontal plane of influence created by the four points. Vishnu, as harbinger of the vertical, seeks to make sense of the mysteries of Shiva as messenger of the horizontal.

It is possible to survive within the space of the four points and not to be aware of the significance of the contraction and extension of the fifth point. But in order for the dual *meaning* of the fifth point to appear (the line essentially as a dual object), the four points have to disappear: a condition for catastrophic change. The fifth point is zenith, the sun as portal to a transformation in dimension: but an idea of the nadir is incipient within the zenith; and with it, the idea of a line, the *axis mundi* as an object dual in meaning, both negation and plenitude, Bion's beam of darkness, or a beam of light. Lineage, thought Hocart (1954: 77), begins with a *dead* king. *Dead* divine kings or *living* divine kings, both with powers of creation, personify the *axis mundi* in either of its aspects.

In traditional cosmology, the four points categorise creation, whether in its positive or negative aspect, according to four divisions. In Hindu belief the four points are sacred texts. But they can be bodily parts: heads or wombs—in particular, the heads and wombs of the heart, or the eyes and ears of the imagination.

Kolam, cave, and temple as observatories of the imagination. In Paul Mus's view, an idea of time motivates conceptions of space in the sacred art of India. Pulse brings into existence a coincidence that is so fleeting that it offers little more than a conjecture about the possible existence of location. The imagination is not "of this world"; and yet it is "in the actual world", in the sense in which a horizon is an actuality in being an imagined intermediary between sky and earth. A cord-source of nimbus, or halo, relates the cranium of the newborn to a celestial realm. But the authority of the cord, as beam of light, depends on its primary meaning as beam of darkness. Without the cosmos in negation there would be no cosmos in plenitude: catastrophe, the inauspicious, underlies any fullness in being. Coincidence, a touch in the night, the easily dispersed mark of a footprint mark the change from negation into plenitude. The Buddha Shakyamuni, at one stage in his life, wished to leave no recollection of himself in the world, apart from a footprint. The threshold, the cranial cord, and the footprints mark loss and remembrance and invoke the remedy of geometric forms.

The nature of imaginative coincidence opposes commonsense assumptions about habitation. In Shakespeare's *The Tempest*, a non-existent king *beneath water* enacts transformations. (The "pearls that were his eyes" are, from another point of view, refractors of the imaginative that bring into being actual eyes.) A ray of light touches the image of a god in the cave. The flickering light of a tallow candle passes over images of animals on the walls of a Palaeolithic cave. An unformed foetus might "think" in this way about its state of immersion in an oceanic and imaginary matrix. It may have intimations of Spinoza's *existence itself* in the fleeting presence of coincidence, even though it may be without the equilibrium that locates presences "out there". Out of *that which is not*, the principle of axiality manifests itself as a beam of darkness as well as a beam of light, indicating the meeting that never occurred, the horizon-threshold never crossed. Out of a seeming nothingness arises geometric form. West African mothers, who think of their newborns as gifts from the sky, arrange gently to lower the infant in the act of birth, so that the newborn's head touches the ground and meets with the two rising shadows of female and male gender.[12]

Shaft and facet.   Shaft and a facet are basic constituents of the *axis mundi*. There can be *one* shaft and *multiple* facets or *multiple* shafts and *one* facet. The Sarnath pillar and the Bayon towers translate shaft and facet into concepts of body and head. There are *multiple* heads and *one* body, or there are *one* head and *multiple* bodies. The sacrificial post, the linga, the throne of the divine king are faceted shafts between heaven and earth. "Head" is a shorthand for "fifth point", the "centre" that is inseparable from cataclysm. "Having a heart" or "having an imagination" (the fifth dimension) is what the visitors to the land of Oz were looking for, without realising its cost.[13]

Patrilineal.   The means by which the rites of sacrifice symbolise cataclysm are either patrilineal or matrilineal. A process of condensation characterises the patrilineal: rites associated with the sacrifice draw everything into themselves. On the Ruvo *kratér*, for instance (see above; also chapters 15, 20), the sacrificer and sacrificed are enigmatically equated in the form of a Janus-headed figure, which is instrumental in symbolising time. One king must die in order that somebody else might be initiated into kingship. The concept of head originates a concept of time (the beginning of the new year as a "head"). Eating the heart, or head, of the old king, or the "head" of the old year, endows an initiate king with sovereignty.[14]

"One body and multiple heads" transforms into "multiple bodies and one head". In the case of one body and multiple heads, the *axis mundi* occurs as a *spatial* means by which a "gaze" can be directed to every quarter. In the case of multiple bodies and one head, the *axis mundi* occurs as a *temporal* means of linking generations through the transitions of birth and death. Reversing the Janus-headed structure brings out the meaning of the Janus-head symbol's relation to time. The *axis mundi* marks out the significance of generation. A young man relegates an "elderly" face to his father or a father donates a "youthful" face to his son. One headless body passes a head on to another headless body. A father takes into him the sorrow and evil of the world (often linked to the ageing of the year's end), while granting joy and fertility to his son. At this point father and son are able to separate.

Matrilineal.   From the patrilineal viewpoint, the matrilineal is a "mother"–sphinx, who is identified with death and deformity: the very idea of the riddle itself. But in order for this misconception to occur, the matrilineal has to remain concealed within the patrilineal structure. If it should free itself, it dissolves personification into the wandering and geometric line of the *kolam*. Time then motivates the qualities of spatial representation. Those who worship the "female principle" as a "personification of universal energy in the abstract" (Rao, 1914: 327) are inclined to practice rites of breathing (*yoga*) and to describe the intensified states of being, acquired by breathing rites, in terms of sacred geometric diagrams, the *yantras* or *chakras*.

In South India, women alone have the prerogative to draw on the ground, often by thresholds, the geometric patterns of the *kolam*. Time motivates these patterns, whether in the form of breathing, or interrupted breathing (the threshold as gap between life and death or death and life). At dusk, after the sun has set, and yet before nightfall, women prepare the ground on which they will draw the pattern, and early the next morning, during the period of first light, before the sun itself appears, they draw the pattern, usually in the form of a single uninterrupted line. First light is the time of the sacrifice and of temporal renewal. Patterning, made by way of a continuous line, counteracts the disease, death, and misfortune associated with *margali*, the last month of the year, in which the cosmos in negation must be challenged.[15]

While the patrilineal loses itself in laconic utterances about death, the matrilineal responds to death expansively, by discovering in it the act of birth and the wayward passions associated with parturition. Nicholas Malebranche (in Rodis-Lewis, 1979: 173–192) was not alone in bitterly asserting that a pregnant woman who looked with passion on the body of somebody other would be punished for the deforming powers of lust—in that such a mother would give birth to a deformed foetus. "Deforming the foetus" is a way of describing the role of catastrophic change in generating the imaginative.

In the throes of jealousy, Shiva fails to recognise the nature of the love that Parvati, his wife, and Ganesh, his newborn son, feel for each other. He accuses Parvati of infidelity and decapitates Ganesh. It is husband, rather than wife, who is afflicted by a deformation of desire and haunted by the idea of the missing head. (The Chinese envoy visiting Bayon thought that the missing head on the towers must have been that of Shiva—see above.) Parvati instructs Shiva to replace the head of her child with the head of the first being he might meet, which in effect was a baby elephant. ("Seeing" the baby elephant is like the passionate look that, the bitter person might think, results in deformation.) Shiva provides his son with an elephant's head, and Ganesh metamorphoses into being the most loved of gods. But who might reinstate the whole being of the baby elephant, who has been left headless? The hanged-man motif re-surfaces: a double decapitation must occur, if there is to be a transposition of heads.

Ganesh contains the risk of being the "incomplete", whether as house or year. But he is also the phantom of a murdered child.

> Only the simplest of the South Indian threshold designs have any real connection with the labyrinth motive from which all are sprung. [Two forms are apparent.] These are *pavitram*, signifying a "ring", and *Brahma-mudi*, meaning "Brahma's knot". . . . The connection between the ring and the design said to represent it is symbolic. In what, then, does the symbolism consist? The Sanskrit root for *pavitram* is *pu*, of which the two allied meanings are: (a) "to cleanse", a meaning doubtless pregnant with spiritual intent, referable in this case presumably to the month of sickness during which the designs are made; and (b) "to pacify", here referable to the god Ganesa, "Leader of Imps" and "Lord of Obstacles", both physical and spiritual, whose month this is. The object of the *pavitram* is to scare away giants, evil spirits, or devils, whose mission it is to bring disasters upon men and mar the ceremonies of the Brahmins. [Layard, 1937: 136–138]

The beam of light gives rise to a type of god whose role as creator does not absorb the resonance of the god's personality, while the beam of darkness gives rise to a type of god whose role as creator absorbs any personality that the god might have had. Brahma, as author of the cosmos in negation, disappears into one of the *kolam* patterns known as the "Brahma knot". Brahmins turn the "Brahma knot" in their hands in prayer.

A cave-temple in Basavangudi.   Raising a king towards the sun by way of a (sacrificial) post or by a throne, or by his being raised to a mountain-peak, restores the unity of the cord that has been severed. But the unity of the cord can be restored also, if the sun's light-rays should transfigure by its fleeting touch an obscure and inward image of the king. "The Shri Gavi Gangdhareshwara Temple in Basavangudi, Bangalore, is a cave temple that demonstrates the ingenuity of ancient architects. Each year on the day of Makara Sankranti (14/15 Jan) the rays of the sun pass between the horns of the stone bull in the temple courtyard and illuminate Gangaharaswamy, a deity who presides over the dark sanctum. The catacombs in the cave temple contain 33 idols. The *"thrishola"* (trident) and the *"damaruga"* (drum) associated with Lord Shiva have been carved out of granite and are seen in the yard outside the cave-temple, and with them are images of *"suryapaana"* (sun) and *"chandrapaana"* (moon)."[16]

The touch of the sun is auspicious; but there is no escaping the dualism by which the auspicious is founded in the inauspicious. All planets are liable to revert to a condition of negation. Plenitude must be worked for by way of a specific magic. Small blackened statues of the nine planetary deities, the *Navagrahas,* stand on a table–altar in one of the side chapels to the cave–temple. "The *Navagrahas* are found in every Shiva-temple. They must be so arranged that no one figure faces the other. They are always in a group together, but each one can be the object of special attention One must avoid having any fixed constellation" (Diehl, 1956: 299). "Attaching the influence of the stars and planets to demons or deities makes them approachable. *When the planets have been turned into gods, they can be negotiated with"* (Diehl, ibid.: 304).

The *Navagrahas* are evocative of the dismembered limbs of Prajâpati, after the first act of sacrifice. A geometric form on the wall behind the small blackened statues corresponds to them in meaning. The geometric form is a *svastika,* a version of the *axis mundi,* or labyrinth, whose relevance as a solar symbol in this context is unaffected by its later Nazi use. As points on the *svastika,* the nine planetary gods assume the form of vertices, junctures in the angles of diamond refraction. Geneviève Haag

(1995) has described proprioceptive junctures in the body in terms of phantasies concerning "eyes" in the body; the gods as points are similar. They might be points of light in the night sky. Conceivably, they personify the formation of insight as it arises from the refractors of the imagination. The points of refraction, which increase the intensity of the light-rays that pass through it, can be seen either as gods or as interpretations.

The plot of land outside the gates to the cave–temple, on which nine trees grow, has the appearance of a shrine. Here the gods assume the form of trees, each of which bears witness to one of the nine planets. A shrine devoted to Nagas, or serpent-gods, lies beneath the trees. Images of two snakes intertwined about the infant Krishna occur among the icons—they bear a resemblance to icons of footprints (whether of Vishnu or the Buddha Shakyamuni), and to the *chakra*, or sacred wheel, imprinted on the footprint. There is also an image of a Naga lying in a shallow tiled ditch.

> According to a familiar legend, the so-called spectacle marks [on the hood of a cobra] are the footprints left by Krishna on the heads of the Naga Kaliya, saying *When Garuda sees my footprints marked on your heads, he will not assail you.*
>
> Sometimes the Nagas are adorned with a svastika or mystic cross. Here again we may think of the spectacle mark [on the hood of the cobra]. [Vogel, 1926: 27]

The relevance of the relationship of trees, snakes, and footprints is apparent in some of the iconography associated with the birth of the Buddha Sakyamuni. Tree shapes intimate the swaying body of his mother, Maya, as she holds onto a tree while giving birth to him (Berthier, 1997). It is as though they reflected the descent of the foetus within her.

> Queen Maya gave birth to the future Buddha in the Lumbini Garden. Nanda and Upananda, two Naga-rajas, appeared. Standing in the air, "half-bodied", the two Naga-rajas produced streams of water, cold and warm, with which they bathed the Bodhisattva. In a bas-relief from Amaravati, Maya is shown standing in the traditional attitude under the tree, while at her side four deities hold up a long piece of cloth to receive the invisible child. Two females, one carrying a

kerchief *marked with the sacred footprints*[17] and the other holding a parasol over it, hasten towards a cistern from which issues a male figure, hands joined in adoration. This figure represents a Naga in his cistern.... In a [similar] Mathura sculpture, some musical instruments floating in the air indicate the heavenly music which was heard at the time of the birth. [Vogel, 1926: 95–96]

In south-east Asia and China, the Indian Nagas or serpent-gods can take the form of water-serpents, dragons, or crocodiles. In opposition to cultures in which the king's identification with the sun is a source of authority, other cultures, sometimes maritime, think of the king as acquiring authority through an identification with the gods, saints, and kings of the watery depths, who may be Nagas (Przyluski, 1925: 283). The royal touch of the sun animates the image of the god-king within the cave–temple; but by way of the planetary trees (the *axis mundi*), the divine Nagas endow the god-king with power also.[18]

The notion of the heavens or the earth as two-dimensional surfaces on which patterns may appear (perhaps imperceptibly) is evocative of the belief that the Holy Spirit, inspiration itself, can be represented by a caesura of indefinite space, which divides the sacred space of temple or cosmos into the circle of the sacrifice and the circle of divination. It is able, by this division, to transform the meaning of the sacrifice into the meaning of a revelation, by whose signs the future speaks to the present. Inspiration, as the dynamic of the imagination, reverses the flow of time, so that time, instead of moving from past into present, moves from the future into the present and by this means liberates itself from the tyranny of duration. An act of liberation of this kind is fundamental to the significance of the two-dimensional *kolam*, as it is to the three-dimensional architecture of the temple.

The symbolism underlying the "loop" *kolams* can be inferred [from] designs which end in snake heads or snakehoods. In all probability the loop *kolam* was derived from snake *kolams*, though its symbolism has generally been forgotten. It can substantiated by representations of snakes (Skt. *néga*) in temples as well as by the very popular Naga cult of South

India, a cult involving the planting of stones dedicated to snakes under sacred trees such as the pippala or asvadha (Skt. *ficus Religiosa*) and the nim or nimba (Skt. *Melia Azadirachta*). We see them also in the vicinity of temple tanks and in sacred groves. On these stones are representations of a snake couple which, entwined in the act of copulation, encloses a small figure (apparently that of Krishna), most probably an allusion to a desired child. Women whose wish for a child has been fulfilled offer snake stones. The snake motif in *kolam* art can be attributed to the magic–apotropaic character of the snake—its association with cure, life, rebirth, and immortality, as well as with disease, death, and destruction. As such the snake is worshipped as a tutelary deity. [Steinmann, 1989: 478]

A popular symbol in *kolam* design is the svastika (Skt.) and its many variations, either turning to the right or to the left. It was known to many ancient cultures as a symbol of the sun and of fertility and as a symbol standing for auspiciousness in general. [ibid.: 479]

The *kolam*, like the *Navagrahas*, is an instrument that transforms negation into plenitude. The patterning of the *kolam* is like a fisherman's net outspread on the sea, which catches in its trawls images of infancy.

While Shiva slept in the forest, Parvati took a piece of wood and drew a *kolam* on the ground. In the *kolam* she placed a fort, a king, Brahmans untouchables, & etc. Shiva woke just at the point at which she had finished the drawing. He asked her why she had invented a city rather than slept. Shiva gave life to the city which became Shivanandapuri. [Biardeau, 1989: 114]

Coleridge's image for the poetic symbol is a harp through which wind or water moves, creating a plangent music. The *kolam* is another such image for the poetic symbol.[19] The unpredictable—a wind that bloweth where it listeth—brings the poetic symbol into being.

Sun and cave. The architecture of the sacred space of the cave–temple of Shri Gavi Gangdhareshwara in Basavangudi articulates a myth that, in terms of motifs, is structurally analogous to the myth of the sun and the cave in Plato's *Republic*, Book 7.[20] But on this score the significance that Plato draws from the sun and cave myth negates any meaning to the concept of *axis mundi*.

The sign system by which Plato's sun communicates is cataclysmic as well as revelatory; in this Plato is no different from the Indian mythologists. But Plato shows how, within the cave, the authorities use the light of fire to promote delusion: he does not see the fire as a god of the sacrifice. He allows for no connection between the solar light *outside* the cave and the light *within* the cave created by fire. He appears to sever any possible link between light outside and light inside the object. In his version of the myth, the temple-matrix has the form of a shell.

The pilgrim who is blinded by having to look into the sun and the cave dwellers who are bound in ignorance are similar in being violated beings. Neither of them is allowed the redemptive value of axiality; and without axial coincidence, the interior of the cave cannot be transfigured into a site for imaginative truth. It is not apparent whether Plato found this type of thinking disagreeable, or whether he was unaware of it. An iconography of a holy sepulchre kind, in which the cosmic space of negation can become the cosmic space of plenitude, is present only as an absence in his thought.[21]

Some distinction between forms of destructive light within and without an object, one being related to truth and the other to falsehood, informs his conception of the icon as an object that arouses his distrust as well as his fascination. The *axis mundi*, insofar as it exists in his myth, is a goad. The cave dwellers are in a state of disablement or, if the cave is viewed as a version of the wandering womb, convulsed. There is neither surcease nor regeneration as functions of the imagination. The Indian cave–temple is an eye-matrix or axial that transforms threshold into pattern and then into mass.[22] Plato's cave is a matrix in which the radiance and warmth of solar fire promotes delusion. Implicit in either case is the presumption that the eye-matrix in the foetus (a metaphysical understanding of Bion's optic pit) has to undergo catastrophic change at some stage that precedes the act of birth itself.

Notes

My thanks to Dawn Rooney for comments on an earlier draft of this chapter.

1. I have observed in Myanmar people kneeling in temple compounds and staring into the sun. Presumably these sun-worshippers soon go blind.

2. It is not unlike the furnace through which Shadrach and his companions were able to pass.

3. *Atharvaveda Samhita*, 10.7.22.

4. It is not an isolated location "out there". It is only *seemingly* a point in space around which the ego forms. Theories concerning the existence of an ego, and of the ego as having a nucleus, are acceptable, insofar as they are described as myths.

5. The commitment of seventeenth-century science to the postulate that scientific law is uniform in its universality informs the universality of duration theory. However, this theory cannot be demonstrated, since the idea of the universal is in itself "indistinct" and therefore, according to Descartes's definition of truth, a form of error.

6. It is not surprising that Adam was depressed. Appointed to be gardener in a garden that was in every way perfect, he must have realised that there was nothing for him to do.

7. Consider "masculine" and "feminine" in this context to mark a foetal attempt to categorise and therefore to be able to think about the imponderable presence of a combined object, which is a source of the power of catastrophic change.

8. Snodgrass (1985: 21) describes the Sanskrit *nahbi* as centre or navel. It is also a space with the property of being expansive.

9. An expert diamond cutter can cut the facets in such a way that light which is reflected onto the diamond is thrown back again—with increased brilliance—by the same route. That is why the stone sparkles. The analyst . . . hopes to reflect back the same illumination given him by the analysand, but with greater intensity (Bion, 1980: 15). It would be a presumption to assume that the "expert diamond cutter" is the analyst. The expert diamond cutter is some agent for *existence itself*, manifesting itself as the future. "A *yantra* [or sacred image] takes on any significance when it becomes the focal point of a devotee's powers of concentration" (Zimmer, 1926: 28 et seq.). Bion's diamond is a form of *yantra* or mandala.

10. Kramrisch (1981: 250 et seq.) sees the missing fifth head as eternity in relation to the four aspects of time represented by the other heads.

11. The patterning in *kolams* intimates the configuration of the sacrificed god. The "labyrinth" created in space by Ariadne's dance movements is like a sea-net that trawls for lost infants.

12. And this is a clue as to why, in Indian thought, the icon of the sacred footprint resembles the icon of the Nagas, or snakes, intertwined about an image of the infant Krishna.

13. Myth by its very existence indicates that *axis mundi* is a means to describe an orientation in time and space before ears and eyes have formed. Like the contact barrier, or zero function (on each side of which are

number series that are either positive or negative), the *axis mundi* shadows forth a combined-object distinction, possibly a distinction in gender.

14. Paying one's dues is a cogent way of describing the year's end.

15. But compare—"The *kolam* design in rice flour is drawn outside the house every morning, except during a time of mourning. Apart from signifying that all is well in the house, it is also a charm against evil spirits. There should never be loose ends, all the lines must meet, so that the evils are captured inside the *kolam* and not permitted to enter. This feat is performed by the snake, whose sinuous coils provide the basis for the patterns" (Krishna, 1992).

16. My thanks to Messrs Natraj and Manohar for providing me with this information.

17. This description makes it clear that some image of womb/placenta is the source of the signs of revelation that mark carvings of the Buddha's footprint. The infant in transit from one breast to the other mediates on the alternation of imaginary geometric forms which a conjunction of a gaze and a feeding object signify. In turn, its speculations about a glance and a nourishment inform belief concerning the nature of some utmost seclusion in its mother's life. Aspects of this seclusion manifest themselves as signs of revelation on a plane surface. The marks on the Buddhas' footprint are such signs of revelation.

18. The theme of the sacrifice brings out an otherwise buried comparison between serpent and tree cults. In my view, the serpent in Asian cults indicates the moment of conception: at the same time, the symbolism of the seed in transformation can take the part-object form of penis–baby or be the radiance of the newborn. According to this thesis, our first parents were expelled from the garden because our first mother became pregnant without divine permission. The symbol of the child–serpent is open in its radiance, while the tree symbol is ambiguous and equivocal.

Various solutions have been proposed for the problematic of the tree in the garden of Eden. Frazer thought that the Genesis legends confused a tree of life and death with a tree that communicates knowledge of good and evil. But if the tree were not problematic, it would not exist: it represents the idea of an insoluble complexity. It is sacrificial post, linga, and *axis mundi*: a site on which murder is dissimulated and projected (the theory of the scapegoat) as well as enacted; and out of its meanings as a symbol emerge the poetics of tragedy. In the New Testament the tree takes the form of what Christians call *the mystery of the cross,* which asks: *why time, why death?* while the serpent carries the transparent significance of Christ. The tree asks: How does the combined object dispose of the desire to kill, or how does it mediate the desire to kill? As tree is to serpent, so time is to eternity. The nature of the link is the symbolism known as iconic.

19. The poetic symbol is inexhaustible in meaning because it is structured to receive the mysterious instructions of inspiration. All poetic symbols are agents for the Holy Spirit.

20. It is possible in the case of both caves to interpret the cave as a kind of mouth that experiences the feeding object as a solar warmth. The mouth–cave, extending down the throat, leads into serpentine depths.

21. Iconographies of a holy sepulchre kind resort to the poetic symbol of the microcosmic divine king's body as the means by which macrocosm transforms negation into plenitude. Here is a possible model for the means by which auricular and optic pits become the ear and eye of the imagination.

22. The massive bull statue in the bull temple next to the cave–temple has a *kolam* in rice powder extending from the side of it. Likewise a figure on a stele in the garden to the National Museum in Bangalore has a pattern extending out of it. Out of the void appears a geometric form, and out of the geometric form appears the three-dimensional, in the form of an impressive mass.

References & Bibliography

Alexandre, P. (Ed.) (1972). *French Perspectives in African Studies.* London: Oxford University Press.

Allen, J. P. (1988). *Genesis in Egypt.* New Haven, CT: Yale University Press.

Assmann, J. (2000). *Images et rites de la mort dans l'Égypte ancienne.* Paris: Cybele.

Bakhtin, M. M. (1968). *Rabelais and His World.* Cambridge, MA: MIT Press.

Barnes, J. (Ed.) (1984). *The Complete Works of Aristotle* (2 vols.). Princeton, NJ: Princeton University Press.

Berthier, F. (1997). L'arbre et la femme. In: J. Pigeot & H. O. Rotermund (Eds.), *Le vase de béryl. Études sur le Japon et la Chine en hommage à Bernard Frank.* Arles: Picquier.

Biardeau, M. (1981). *Études de mythologie hindoue. Vol. 1: Cosmogonies puraniques.* Paris: École Française d'Extrême-Orient.

Biardeau, M. (1989). *Histoires de poteaux: Variations védiques autour de la Déesse hindoue.* Paris: École Française d'Extrême-Orient.

Bion, W. R. (1970). *Attention and Interpretation.* London: Tavistock.

Bion, W. R. (1973). *Brazilian Lectures.* London: Karnac, 1990.

Bion, W. R. (1980). *Bion in New York and São Paolo.* Strathtay: Clunie Press.

Blier, S. P. (1995). *African Vodun.* Chicago, IL: University of Chicago Press.

Bomhard, A. -S. von (1999). *The Egyptian Calendar: A Work for Eternity.* London: Periplus.

Calame-Griaule, G. (1965). *Ethnologie et langage: la parole chez les Dogon.* Paris: Institut d'Ethnologie, 1987.

Cartry, M. (1963). Notes sur les signes graphiques du géomancien gourmantché. *Journal de la Société des Africanistes, 33* (2): 275–306.

Cartry, M. (1976). Le statut de l'animal dans le système sacrificiel des Gourmantché (Haute-Volta), Part 1. In: *Systèmes de pensée en Afrique noire. Book 2: Le sacrifice I* (pp. 141–175). Paris: C.N.R.S.

Cartry, M. (1978). Le statut de l'animal dans le système sacrificiel des Gourmantché (Haute-Volta), Part 2. In: *Systèmes de pensée en Afrique noire. Book 3: Le sacrifice II* (pp. 7–58). Paris: C.N.R.S.

Cartry, M. (1981). Le statut de l'animal dans le système sacrificiel des Gourmantché (Haute-Volta), Part 3. In: *Systèmes de pensée en Afrique noire. Book 5: Le sacrifice IV* (pp. 195–216). Paris: C.N.R.S.

Char, R. (1944). *Fureur et mystère.* Paris: Gallimard, 1962.

Chelhod, J. (1954). Le monde arabe examiné a la lumière d'un mythe africain. *Journal de la Société des Africanistes, 24*: 1.

Cissé, Y. (1973). Signes graphiques, représentations, concepts et tests relatifs à la personne chez les Malinké et les Bambaras du Mali. In: *La notion de personne en Afrique Noir.* Paris: Éditions l'Harmattan.

Cissé, Y. (1985). Les nains et l'origine des *boli* de chasse chez les Malinké. In: *Systèmes de pensée en Afrique noir. Book 8: Fétiches.* Paris: C.N.R.S.

Clark, G. (Transl. & Ed.) (1989). *Iamblichus: On the Pythagorean Life.* Liverpool: Liverpool University Press.

Cœdès, G. (1943). *Pour mieux comprendre Angkor.* Paris: Librairie d'Amérique et d'Orient, Adrien Maisonneuve.

Cook, A. B. (1904). Zeus, Jupiter and the Oak. *Classical Review,* *18.*

Coomaraswamy, A. K. (1938). The Symbolism of the Dome. *Indian Historical Quarterly, XIV.* In: R. Lipsey (Ed.), *The Selected Papers of A. K. Coomaraswamy, Vol. 1: Traditional Art and Symbolism* (pp. 415–464). Bollingen Series. Princeton, NJ: Princeton University Press, 1977.

Coomaraswamy, A. K. (1939). Svayamâtrnnâ: Janua Coeli. In: R. Lipsey (Ed.), *The Selected Papers of A. K. Coomaraswamy, Vol. 1: Traditional Art and Symbolism* (pp. 465–520). Bollingen Series. Princeton, NJ: Princeton University Press, 1977.

Coomaraswamy, A. K. (1947). *Time & Eternity.* New Delhi: Munshiram Manoharial, 2001.

Cornford, F. M. (1937). *Plato's Cosmology.* London: Kegan Paul.

Cottingham, J., Stoothoff, R., & Murdoch, D. (Transl.) (1984). *The Philosophical Writings of Descartes.* Cambridge: Cambridge University Press.

Cushing, F. H. (1896). Outlines of Zuñi Creation Myths. Thirteenth Annual Report of the Bureau of American Ethnology, 1891–1892. Washington, D.C. In: J. Green (Ed.), *Zuñi: Selected Writings of Frank Hamilton Cushing.* Lincoln, NB: University of Nebraska Press, 1979.

Dakari, M. (1985). *Dionysos et la déesse terre.* Paris: Les Editions Arthaud; Paris: Flammarion, 1994.

Dallapicolla, A. (Ed.) (1989). *Shastric Traditions in Indian Arts.* Wiesbaden: Franz Steiner.

Dasen, V. (1993). *Dwarfs in Ancient Egypt and Greece.* Oxford: Clarendon Press.

Deedes, C. N. (1935). The Double-Headed God. *Folklore, 46.*

Derrida, J. (1967). *De la grammatologie.* Paris: Éditions de Minuit.

Diehl, C. G. (1956). *Instrument and Purpose: Studies on Rites and Rituals in South India.* Lund: Gleerup.

Dieterlen, G. (1950). *Essai sur la religion bambara.* Paris: Presses Universitaires de France. Reprinted Brussels: Editions de l'université de Bruxelles, 1988.

Dieterlen, G. (1952) [with M. Griaule]. Signes d'écriture bambara. In: *Signes graphiques soudanais.* Paris: Herman. Les Cahiers de l'Homme.

Dieterlen G. (1965). A Contribution to the Study of Blacksmiths in West Africa. In: P. Alexandre (Ed.), *French Perspectives in African Studies*. London: Oxford University Press, 1972.

Dieterlen, G., & Cissé, Y. (1972). *Les Fondements de la société d'initiation du Komo*. Paris: Mouton.

Dodds, E. R. (1951). *The Greeks and the Irrational*. Berkeley, CA: University of California Press.

Dumézil, G. (1971). *Mythe et épopée. Vol. 2: The Destiny of a King* (transl. by A. Hiltebeitel). Chicago, IL: Chicago University Press, 1973.

Eggeling, J. (Transl.) (1894). *The Satapatha-Brâhmana*. Oxford: Clarendon Press.

Erman, A., & Grapow, H. (1992). *Wörterbuch der ägyptischen Sprache* (12 vols.). Berlin: Akademie Verlag, Nachdruck.

Faulkner, R. O. (Transl.) (1973). *The Ancient Egyptian Coffin Texts, Vol. 1: Spells 1–354*. Warminster: Aris & Phillips.

Frankfort, H. (1933). *The Cenotaph of Seti I at Abydos* (2 vols.). London: The Egypt Exploration Society.

Frédéric, L. (1995). *Buddhism* (transl. by N. Marshall). Paris: Flammarion.

Freud, S. (1911b). Formulations on the Two Principles of Mental Functioning. *S.E. 12*.

Freud, S. (1913f). The Theme of the Three Caskets. *S.E. 12*.

Freud, S. (1918b [1914]). From the History of an Infantile Neurosis. *S.E. 17*.

Freud, S. (1923b). *The Ego and the Id. S.E. 22*.

Freud, S. (1933a). *New Introductory Lectures on Psycho-Analysis. S.E. 22*.

Freud, S. (1941f [1938]). Findings, Ideas, Problems. *S.E. 23*.

Freud, S. (1950 [1896]). Draft K. The Neuroses of Defence (A Christmas Fairy Tale). *S.E. 1*.

Granet, M. (1926). *Danses et légendes de la Chine ancienne*. Paris: Presses Universitaires de France, 1994.

Graves, R. (1948). *Collected Poems 1914–1947*. London: Cassell.

Griaule, M. (1937). Notes sur la divination par le chacal. *Bulletin du Comité d'etudes historiques et scientifiques de l'Afrique occidentale française, 20*.

Griaule, M. (1938). *Masques dogons*. Paris: Institut d'Ethnologie, 1983.

Griaule, M. (1948). *Dieu l'Eau, Entretiens avec Ogotemmêli*. Paris: Fayard, 1966.

Griaule, M., & Dieterlen, G. (1950). La Harpe-luth des Dogon. *Journal de la Société des Africanistes, 20* (2).

Griaule, M., & Dieterlen, G. (1965). *Le renard pâle*. Paris: Institute d'Ethnologie, 1991.

Haag, G. (1995). Comment l'esprit vient au corps. In: M.-B. Lacroix & M. Monmayrant, *Les liens d'ermerveillement*. Ramonville St-Agne: Éditions Érès.

Haberland, E. (Ed.) (1973). *Leo Frobenius: An Anthology*. Wiesbaden: Franz Steiner.

Hannig, R. (1995). *Handwörterbuch Ägyptisch-Deutsch. Kulturgeschichte der antiken Welt, Vol. 64*. Mainz: Verlag Philipp von Zabern.

Heusch, L. de (1987). *Ecrits sur la royauté sacrée*. Brussels: Éditions de l'Université de Bruxelles.

Heusch, L. de (1990). Introduction. In: *Systèmes de pensée en Afrique noir, Vol. 10: Chefs et Rois sacrés*. Paris: C.N.R.S.

Heusch, L. de (2000). *Le roi de Kongo et les monstres sacrés*. Paris: Gallimard.

Himmelheber, H. (1963). Personality and Technique of African Sculptors. In: *Lecture Series Number Three: Technique and Personality in Primitive Art*. New York: Museum of Primitive Art.

Hjelmslev, L. (1971). *Essais Linguistiques*. Paris: Éditions de Minuit.

Hocart. A. M. (1954). *Social Origins*. London: Watts.

Isakower, O. (1939). On the exceptional position of the auditory sphere. *International Journal of Psycho-Analysis, 20*: 340–348.

Jespers, P. (1976). Contribution à l'étude des autels sacrificiels du Nya chez les Minyanka du Mali. In: *Systèmes de pensée en Afrique noire. Book 2: Le sacrifice I* (pp. 111–139). Paris: C.N.R.S.

Jespers, P. (1979). Signes graphiques minyanka. *Journal de la Société des Africanistes, 49* (1): 71–102.

Kante, N. (1993). *Forgerons d'Afrique noire*. Paris: L'Harmattan.

Kirk, G. S, Raven, J. E., & Schofield, M. (1957). *The Presocratic Philosophers*. Cambridge: Cambridge University Press, 1983.

Kitzinger, E. (1954). The Cult of Images in the Age before Iconoclasm. *Dumbarton Oaks Papers, 8*.

Koyré, A. (1957). *From the Closed World to the Infinite Universe.* Baltimore, MD: Johns Hopkins University Press.

Kramrisch, S. (1946). *The Hindu Temple.* Calcutta: University Press; Delhi: Banarsidass, 1976.

Kramrisch, S. (1981). *The Presence of Shiva.* Princeton, NJ: Princeton University Press.

Krautheimer, R. (1942). Introduction to an "Iconography of Mediaeval Architecture". *Journal of the Warburg and Courtauld Institutes, 5.*

Krishna, N. (1992). *Arts and Crafts of Tamilnadu.* Ahmedabad: Mapin.

Ladner, G. B. (1953). The Concept of the Image in the Greek Fathers and the Byzantine Iconoclastic Controversy. *Dumbarton Oaks Papers, 7.*

Ladner, G. B. (1979). Medieval and Modern Understanding of Symbolism. *Speculum, 54.* In: G B. Ladner, *Images and Ideas in the Middle Ages. Selected Studies in History and Art, Vol. 1.* Rome: Edizioni di Storia e Letteratura, 1983.

Ladner, G. B. (1983). *Images and Ideas in the Middle Ages. Selected Studies in History and Art.* Rome: Edizioni di Storia e Letteratura.

Layard, J. (1937). Labyrinth Ritual in South India: Threshold and Tattoo Designs. *Folklore, 48.*

Lebeuf, A. M. D. (1973). Le personnage du roi et les structures spatio-temporelles. In: *La Notion de personne en Afrique noire.* Paris: Éditions l'Harmattan.

Leibniz, G. W. von (1675). *Sämtliche Schriften und Briefe, Series 6, Vol. 3.* Berlin: Akademie Verlag, 1980.

Lévi-Strauss, C. (1944). *Le Dédoublement de la représentation dans les arts de l'Asie et de l'Amérique.* New York: Renaissance. École libre de Hautes Études. English edition: Split Representation in the Art of Asia and America. In: *Structural Anthropology, Vol. 1.* Harmondsworth: Peregrine, 1963, 1977.

Lévi-Strauss, C. (1950). Introduction à l'oeuvre de Marcel Mauss. In: M. Mauss, *Sociologie et anthropologie.* Quadrige: Presses Universitaires de France. English edition: *Introduction to the Work of Marcel Mauss* (transl. by F. Baker). London: Routledge & Kegan Paul, 1987.

Lévi-Strauss, C. (1956). Les Organisations dualistes existent-elles? English edition: Do Dual Organisations Exist? In: *Structural Anthropology, Vol. 1*. Harmondsworth: Peregrine, 1977.

Lévi-Strauss, C. (1957). Le symbolisme cosmique dans la structure sociale et l'organisation ceremonielle de plusieurs populations Nord et Sud-Americaines. In: *Le Symbolisme cosmique des monuments religieux*, Serie Orientale Roma. Rome: Istituto Italiano per il Medio ed Estremo Oriente.

Lévi-Strauss, C. (1958). La geste d'Asdiwal. *Annuaire 1958–1959, Ecole practique des haute études.* English edition in: *Structural Anthropology, Vol. 2* (transl. by M. Layton). Harmondsworth: Penguin Books, 1976.

Lévi-Strauss, C. (1962a). Jean-Jacques Rousseau, fondateur des sciences de l'homme. English edition in: *Structural Anthropology, Vol. 2* (transl. by M. Layton). Harmondsworth: Penguin, 1976.

Lévi-Strauss, C. (1962b). *Le totémisme aujourd'hui*. Paris: Presses Universitaires de France. English edition: *Totemism* (transl. by R. Needham). London: Merlin Press, 1964.

Lichtheim, M. (Transl.) (1975). *Ancient Egyptian Literature. Vol. 1: The Old and Middle Kingdoms*. Berkeley, CA: University of California Press.

Lincoln, B. (1986). *Myth, Cosmos, and Society: Indo-European Themes of Creation and Destruction*. Cambridge, MA: Harvard University Press.

Lipsey, R. (Ed.) (1977). *The Selected Papers of A. K. Coomaraswamy, Vol. 1: Traditional Art and Symbolism*. Bollingen Series. Princeton, NJ: Princeton University Press.

Malamoud, C. (1989). *Cuire le Monde: Rite et pensée dans l'Inde ancienne*. Paris: Éditions la Découverte. English edition: *Cooking the World* (transl. by D. White). Delhi: Oxford University Press, 1996.

Maspero, G. (1893). Sur une formule du Livre des Pyramides. In: *Études de Mythologie et d'Archéologie Égyptiennes, Vol. 2*. Paris: Ernest Leroux.

Maspero, H. (1927). *La Chine antique*. Paris: de Broccard.

Maupoil, B. (1943). *La Géomancie à l'ancienne côte des esclaves*. Paris: Institut d'Ethnologie, 1988.

Mauro, T. de (Ed.) (1972). *Ferdinand de Saussure's Cours de linguistique générale*. Paris: Éditions Payot.

Meister, M. W. (Ed.) (1995). *Ananda K. Coomarswamy: Essays in Architectural Theory*. New Delhi: Oxford University Press.

Meuli, K. (1935). Scythica. *Hermes, 70*. Berlin: Weidmann.

Mus, P. (1933). Cultes indiens et indigènes au Champa. *Bulletin de l'École Française d'Extrême Orient, 33*: 1.

Mus, P. (1935). *Barabudur*. Paris: Arma Artis, 1990.

Pâques, V. (1954). *Les Bambaras*. Paris: Presses Universitaires de France.

Pâques, V. (1977). *Le roi pecheur et le roi chasseur*. Strasbourg: Institute d'Anthropologie.

Parkinson, G. H. R. (Ed.) (1989). *Spinoza, Ethics* (1677). [A revised version of Andrew Boyle's translation.] London: J. M. Dent & Sons.

Paulme, D. (1937). La divination par les chacals chez les Dogon de Sanga. *Journal de la Société des Africanistes, 3*: 1–13.

Piankoff, A., & Rambova, N. (1957). *Mythological Papyri*. New York: Pantheon Books.

Pigeot, J., & Rotermund, H. O. (Ed.) (1997). *Le vase de béryl. Études sur le Japon et la Chine en hommage à Bernard Frank*. Arles: Picquier.

Polotsky, J. (1976). Les transpositions du verbe en egyptien classique. *Israel Oriental Studies, 6*.

Przyluski, J. (1925). La princesse à l'odeur de poisson et la nagi dans les traditions de l'Asie orientale. *Études Asiatiques, 2*.

Rambova, N. (1957). The Symbolism of the Papyri. In: A. Piankoff & N. Rambova, *Mythological Papyri*. New York: Pantheon, 1957.

Rao, G. (1914). *Elements of Hindu Iconography*. Madras: Law Printing House.

Robertson Smith, W. (1894). *The Religion of the Semites*. London: Adam & Charles Black.

Rodis-Lewis, G. (1979). *Malebranche Oeuvres*. Paris: Éditions Gallimard.

Saussure, F. de (1879). *Mémoire sur le système primitif des voyelles dans les langues indo-européennes*. Hildesheim: Georg Olms, 1968.

Saussure, F. de (1916). *Cours de linguistique générale* (ed. by T. de Mauro). Paris: Éditions Payot, 1972.

Shirley, S. (Transl.) (1995). *Spinoza: The Letters*. Indianapolis/Cambridge, MA: Hackett.

Snodgrass, A. (1985). *The Symbolism of the Stupa*. New Delhi: Banarsidass, 1992.

Southall, J. P. C. (Ed.) (1962). *Helmholtz's Treatise on Physiological Optics* (1909). New York: Dover.

Steinmann, R. M. (1989). *Kolam*. Form, technique, and application of a changing folk art of Tamil Nadu. In: A. Dallapicolla (Ed.), *Shastric Traditions in Indian Arts*. Wiesbaden: Franz Steiner.

Tucci, G. (1949). *The Theory and Practice of the Mandala* (transl. by A. H. Broderick). London: Rider, 1961.

Vogel, J. P. (1926). *Indian Serpent Lore or The Nagas in Hindu Legend and Art*. London: Probsthain.

Wainwright, G. A. (1932). Letopolis. *Journal of Egyptian Archeology, 18*.

Wainwright, G. A. (1938). *The Sky-Religion in Egypt*. Cambridge: Cambridge University Press.

West, M. L. (1971). *Early Greek Philosophy and the Orient*. Oxford: Clarendon Press.

Willems, H. (1996). The Shu-Spells in Practice. In: *The World of the Coffin Text. Proceedings of the Symposium Held on the Occasion of the 100th Birthday of Adriaan de Buck*. Leiden: Nederlands Instituut voor het Nabije Oosten.

Zimmer, H. (1926). *Artistic Form and Yoga in the Sacred Images of India*. Princeton, NJ: Princeton University Press, 1948.

Index